❧ conte

1

overview

Sketches

A book on goodness? When the idea was first proposed by the people at Loyola Press, I quickly rejected it. Goodness was a subject far too abstract for a concrete writer like me. But my subconscious apparently thought otherwise, because one morning a short time later I awoke with this sentence in my head: "I had the great good fortune to be reared in a cocoon of goodness." And because this seemed an ideal opening for such a book, I devised a way to deal with the topic. Instead of a philosophical treatise on goodness, I would write sketches of good people I'd known in my life, beginning with those who formed that cocoon around me in my earliest years, namely, my parents and my mother's cousin Bunny.

Writing about my parents in this first chapter led me to ponder an interesting distinction between goodness of a natural sort—that is, kindness that grows out of a person's instinctive, generous character—and what I call "goodness by the book"; that is, being good at the direction of a higher authority, in this case the Catholic Church.

Until I was nearly fifty years old, I thought my parents were alike in their kindness and generosity, at least toward me, but I proved to be mistaken.

The next chapter is about my paternal grandmother and a maternal great-aunt, both of them named Elizabeth, who left their marks on different levels of society, my impoverished grandmother working among the poor of her Midwestern village, while my great-aunt the educator supervised metropolitan teachers in her attempt to civilize two generations of students.

My mother's father deserves a chapter of his own, for he was the one true "character" in my ancestry, a gruff-acting yet jolly man liable at any moment to break into song or break out in a storytelling jag—in contrast to his wife, my grandmother, a fretful woman whose goodness was clouded by worry.

Timmy and Jackie, two friends from my early boyhood, provide an interesting contrast between the bad and the good. One of them was a nine-year-old terrorist who, with my cooperation, masterminded a train derailment, while the other, in the process of dying at the age of twelve, proved himself a saint.

Next the reader will find a chapter devoted to a number of people who entered my life at precisely the right moment to do me a great deal of good. A college professor, for example, who steered me into a life devoted to literature. A colleague who bailed me out of a difficult assignment directing a high-school play. Six colleagues of mine who, together with me, formed a tight bond of friendship in the process of helping one another over the rough places in our early careers as college instructors.

Among the many discoveries I've made in composing these chapters is the realization that there are three geographical locations where I have spent a good bit of time—a village (eight years), a campus (thirty-three semesters), and a lake cabin (twenty-five summers)—and that have become, in retrospect, sacred places for me, due primarily to the good people I have known there.

The eighth chapter is devoted to a rather detailed study of two people, a husband and wife, who struck their colleagues as testy and abrasive but who, upon dying, left behind a legacy of goodness.

The reader may be surprised to find a chapter devoted to certain good characters I have invented in my fiction. Having lived with them in my head for an average of two years each, they have become as real to me as a good many living, breathing human beings of my acquaintance.

Perpetrators of Goodness

And now, having finished these sketches, I see what a narcissistic project it's been. In the first place, to qualify for this book, it isn't enough that the perpetrators of goodness be good; most of them must have been good to me. But I see no alternative. Despite the purity of a person's motive in doing good, it's only the recipient who can determine whether a good act leads to a successful consequence. Having spent forty-two years as a teacher, for example, I like to think that I did my students a lot of good, and yet, whereas perhaps two dozen of them have actually told me so, I have no idea whether the other seven thousand were affected in any lasting way by my efforts.

And second, this book is based on my perceptions alone. I suspect that very few of these people are, or were in their lifetimes, universally thought of as especially virtuous. A storyteller named Michael Cotter once visited my classroom and told a fascinating tale, among others, about a hired man who had died after being employed on the Cotter family farm for many years. The family was mightily grieved, for this man had been not only a faithful worker but a dependable friend to all of them. At his funeral, therefore, they were amazed to meet the man's brothers and sisters, from whom he had been estranged for many years, and to find that he was universally despised by all of them.

This book is by no means an exhaustive study of people I have perceived as virtuous. With each year of my life I seem to become acquainted with more and more good people, until now I am surrounded by literally hundreds of them. The reader will find, too, that almost all my sketches are from the past, for I am able to describe, to shape vignettes around, only those people I have some distance from.

Here, then, is a selected sampling of the many good people who have accompanied me on my journey through life and warmed my heart.

2

my father,
my mother, and
bunny

The Magic of "Mortified"

I had the great good fortune to be reared in a cocoon of goodness. Born in the depths of the depression (1933) and growing up during World War II, I was scarcely aware of the traumatic events that touched most families, including my own. Poverty was the first trauma of my parents' married life, and the effect of it stretched well into their old age, causing them in their eighties to behave as though they were on the brink of destitution. To the very end of their lives, my mother, for example, hung up her paper towels to dry, and my father, a former grocer, suffered shock every time he entered a market and looked at the prices.

My father was one of the nation's millions of workers out of work when I was born. He and my mother were living with her parents, whose house on a pretty elm-shaded street in Minneapolis was full to overflowing, for my mother's two brothers, John and Edward, both out of work, lived there as well, together with John's wife, Helen. It's a mystery to me how these seven people supported themselves; for my grandfather, then in his mid-sixties, had never been a successful breadwinner since losing his job as conductor on the Milwaukee Road many years earlier. Within half a year of my birth, fortunately, my father secured a position as store manager for a grocery chain, and he, my mother, and I moved to a small town in northern Minnesota, where we spent the first ten years of my life.

When I was two, a fourth person entered our household, coming to us by bus from Montana. This was
Bunny Horner, my mother's fourteen-year-old cousin,
the daughter of an impoverished silver miner. Because
Bunny's real name was Ellen, my mother, meeting her at
the bus, asked, "Will we call you Bunny or Ellen?"

"Oh, call me Bunny. I hate the name Ellen, don't you?"

"Not in the least," said my mother, whose name
happened to be Ellen.

Surely this was the last awkward moment between
them, for they became the closest of friends, united
primarily, I think, by their matching senses of humor.
Bunny lived with us throughout her high-school years,
and whenever I call up a memory of that time, I hear
their laughter. I remember, for example, sitting on the
living-room floor—I must have been three or four—and
looking down the hallway toward my parents' bedroom,
where my mother, never an early riser, was still in bed
and visiting with Bunny, who stood in her doorway. (My
father had already left for work.) I can hear again only
one brief phrase of their conversation, repeated several
times by my mother. "I'm mortified," she is saying, and
Bunny laughs. Again and again she says she's mortified
until neither of them can breathe for laughing so hard.
Then Bunny goes off to school, and I am left to contem-
plate the magic of "mortified."

The power of words was only one of several things I
learned from these three good people who doted on me

as a child. The magnetism of stories was another. At least
once a day I was read to by my mother and Bunny, and
on Sunday mornings my father read me the funnies. I
have *The Story of Ferdinand* and *Clementina the Flying Pig*
still in my library (and being enjoyed now by their third
generation of readers), but among my most sacred possessions are A. A. Milne's two slim volumes of poetry,
When We Were Very Young and *Now We Are Six*. These
were the stories that proved unforgettable to me,
heightened as they are by rhythm and rhyme. I've come
to believe, in fact, that every time I write the beginning
of a novel, I'm merely working a variation on the
opening of Milne's "The Four Friends":

> Ernest was an Elephant, a great big fellow,
> Leonard was a lion with a six-foot tail,
> George was a goat and his beard was yellow,
> And James was a very small snail.
>
> Leonard had a stall, and a great big strong one,
> Ernest had a manger and its walls were thick,
> George found a pen but I think it was the wrong one,
> And James sat down on a brick.

Please Your Mother, Please the World

Porky Pig is at least as old as I am. I associate Porky Pig
with movies I saw as a child, and I can still picture him,
at the end of each of his Warner Brothers cartoons,
saying, "Th-th-th-that's all, folks," with the words "Loony
Tunes" written above his head and "Merry Melodies"

below. I pronounced them "Loony tunes and merry moodles," because I was just then learning to read and the phrase never stayed on the screen long enough for me to examine the final word. One day, sitting next to my mother in the theater, I read the phrase aloud, "moodles" rhyming with "noodles," and caused her to laugh with delight, as though this was the funniest thing I'd said up to this point in my life. Rather than feel chagrin at being laughed at, I was pleased with myself for pleasing her. She repeated the phrase a number of times over the next several years, reminding me how clever I could be, even when I was mistaken.

We shared many amusing moments like this, me making small jokes, wittingly or unwittingly, and my mother picking up on them, giving me more credit than I deserved, and encouraging more of the same by storing them in her memory and bringing them into her conversation whenever they seemed pertinent. With encouragement like that when young, how can I help being a writer as an adult? Please your mother, please the world—the two are related.

One morning when I was eleven or twelve, the three of us were riding to Sunday Mass when my father drove us past the local funeral home. There on the sidewalk stood the undertaker, Mike Foley, directing the driver of his hearse as he pulled it up to the curb. Mr. Foley, being a family friend, gave us a broad smile as we passed by, waving at us with one hand as he directed the driver with the other. "Look, there's Mike Foley," said my mother. ". . . so jovial while rigor morting," said I, finishing her sentence for her. Practically for the rest of her long life, she would say, "Jovial while rigor morting" whenever she saw a smiling undertaker—thereby demonstrating to me the power of publication, how the well-turned phrase can be a joy forever if by some means it can be held onto. My mother's memory was the means in those days. Books are my means now.

Two Men in a Boat

A sense of language, a sense of story, and a sense of humor—these three gifts handed down to me primarily by my Irish mother would not have been translated into my (thus far) eleven novels without certain gifts of character I was given by my German father. I'm talking about industry, perseverance, and patience.

Each of my novels has been the work, on average, of two years. At some point in the writing, pausing to consider what I've written and realizing that the final page lies months and maybe even years ahead, I thank God for providing me with a writer's personality. Rather than requiring instant gratification, I find it much more satisfying to toil patiently away at a project over time, every day doggedly creating and revising and showing it to no one until the work is formed to my satisfaction. For this I had my father's example. A kindly, patient, hardworking man, he was my boss as well as my father,

for I spent the summers of my high-school years working with him in the grocery store. This was in the second of my two hometowns, situated in the rich farm-
land of southern Minnesota, where we moved when I
was ten. Six mornings a week, beginning in June 1949,
he would knock on my bedroom door at 7:00 A.M., and
at 7:30 I would still be rubbing the sleep from my eyes
as I freshened the produce rack and waited on the few
customers trickling through the store at that early
hour, and as he sat at his desk tending to his bookwork
before business picked up and he was needed at the
checkout counter.

Like most fathers of that day and age, and unlike my
mother, he had little to say. I recall the two of us sitting
silently in a rowboat while fishing one Sunday afternoon,
and when we got home, my mother's first question wasn't
"What did you catch?" it was "What did you talk about?"

"Fishing," I answered, recalling our discussion about
how deep to dangle our minnows.

"And what else?"

"Nothing else," said my father. "He and I don't need
to talk."

Speech to him, it seemed, was like long-distance
telephone calls in those days, a gift to be used in emer-
gencies. But though we never had much to say to each
other, we somehow formed a very tight bond that lasted
a lifetime. He loved me, even admired me—I could see it
in his smile. When he lay dying for two weeks in the

hospital, I sat at his bedside for hours each day, scribbling changes on the manuscript pages of my novel *A Green Journey.* He spent most of this time sleeping, but occasionally, when he roused himself and turned his head on the pillow to see if I was still there, he'd give me this same smile and drift off again. Nothing had changed between us. We might have been in the rowboat again.

Crippling Blows

My mother was the eldest daughter of the eldest daughter of indigent Irish immigrants, and so had two generations of hard work, religious zeal, and a gradually improving lifestyle to model her own life after. She had a will of steel and lived most of her life with the conviction that all of us were masters of our destiny, and if anyone failed to meet a goal, the problem could probably be traced to a character flaw. But then in her late sixties, she suffered three crippling blows, which she did not have the strength to overcome. The first was delivered by her beloved Catholic Church, the second by my father, the last by me.

She was one of those "ideal" Catholics of days gone by. She loved the liturgy, the rules and regulations, if not all the personnel, of the church. While she might rail against or ridicule any and all churchmen who fell below her standards—perhaps this one was foppish, or that one was senile, or Father So-and-So seemed insincere—she was devoted to the Vatican's system of morality, to its

saint-filled calendar, and above all, to the Mass, with its
lovely bells and candles and music and prayers. There was
an incredible magnificence about all of this, sensual as
well as spiritual, and not one of the five senses was
neglected. There was holy water on the tips of your
fingers, the aroma of incense drifting into your nose,
vestments and statuary and stained glass for your eye,
hymns and chants for your ear, and the grainy taste of
communion on your tongue. All of these pleasures had
been added to the church over centuries, just as moss
and vines adhere to a building over time, clinging and
coloring the brick until you can't be sure where the
understructure stops and the accretion begins.

Then came Vatican II. Meatless Fridays, kneeling
benches, and rosary beads were suddenly out of style.
Prayers were rewritten, altars were relegated to museums
and replaced by what looked like freestanding picnic
tables, and the church calendar was revised to better fit
the needs of modern humankind. The church, of course,
traveling through centuries, must alter its mode of
operation occasionally in order to remain relevant, but
the autocratic suddenness of these changes was shocking
and—to people like my parents—cruel. Overnight, the
faithful were forbidden to hear the type of Mass they
went to yesterday. Priests bent on saying such a Mass
were excommunicated.

I came through this sea change pretty well, though
not without resistance during the first few years. My

father came through it too by not paying any attention to it. Until his death twenty years later, he carried his beads and his outmoded Latin missal to Mass. My mother, however, was devastated. The old ways had been to her not only a guide to behavior, but her hope for salvation, and now she was bereft, disoriented. She continued to attend Sunday Mass, but grudgingly, and she prayed for the return of the old ways. For consolation she turned, during her wakeful nighttime hours, to Dr. Schuler, Billy Joe Hargis, and other evangelists on the radio. "Where are all those people who went to hell for eating meat on Friday?" she was fond of asking bitterly in priestly company.

"Finish Your Jell-O"

While my father relaxed into old age, my mother fought it. She managed by force of will, it seemed, to retain her sharp mind and reliable memory to the end of her ninety-one years, but she couldn't force my father to do the same. As he became more sedentary and less articulate, my mother interpreted his decline as a kind of betrayal, his old age an offense against her high standards of behavior. And, worse, he seemed oblivious to her scolding and sadness. He grew more and more self-satisfied as his natural composure mixed with forgetfulness.

I recall staying overnight with them one time during this phase of their lives. My mother came out of her bedroom in the morning, and finding my father and me silently reading books, she said, "Look at the two of you!" with surprising heat and disgust. My father, engrossed in a historical novel by Anya Seton, was on page 900 and had doubtless forgotten everything up to page 890. He read the way other people breathed, as though the movement of his eyes across the page was what pulled him ahead from one day to the next. "Look at you two spooks!" said Mother, irked by how bookish and unexciting we looked, how neatly I fit my father's passive mold.

How ironic that she who taught us our love of books found fault in our reading them, but her need of talk was greater than her love of the printed page. She knew, of course, that I would very soon be drawn into conversation with her, but these first few minutes—the warm-up time I required—she found intolerable. What I remember most clearly about her family—the Callinans, the Meanys, the O'Malleys—was the spontaneity of their talk. Any two of them coming together needed no time to identify each other's mood or wavelength, but would plunge immediately into happy chatter, underneath which ran the intertwining currents of warmth and humor. What a pity that she couldn't relive those gregarious times with the two men in her life.

Her impatience with my father grew from disgust to alarm. As he went into steeper decline, her scolding became sharper and more persistent. On his last day alive, my mother and I were about to leave his hospital room as his supper was brought in. It was a meal he was not hungry for, and despite her urging him to eat, he consumed only a few small morsels and then laid down his fork and closed his eyes. As we left the room, she said sternly, "Finish your Jell-O." These, after fifty-four years of marriage, were her last words to him.

Goodness by the Book

In 1981, when I was forty-eight years old and she was eighty, everything changed between my mother and me. Although we had been kindred spirits for half a century, she didn't appear to like me anymore. I had divorced my wife of twenty-five years and had then become interested in another woman. Visiting their home one summer afternoon, I found my parents prepared for battle. They took turns warning me away from any and all romantic entanglements. I understood their viewpoint; my marriage had been arduous and unhappy for them as well as for me. They had had to care for my three children for long periods of time during my wife's sieges of depression and her hospitalization. My oldest son, Mike, in fact, had lived with them for ten years. But seeing their viewpoint didn't soften my anger—indeed my panic—and I asked them to keep their noses out of my business. My father seemed fairly unperturbed by my outburst, and on my next visit he greeted me as warmly as before. It would be nine years, however, before a dose of Prozac when she was nearly ninety permitted my mother to smile at me again.

From their separate reactions, I learned the difference between being naturally good and being good by the book. Throughout their long lives, both my father and mother were guided in their behavior by the rules of the Catholic Church. They went to Mass and confession, they gave money in their weekly envelopes, they fasted and prayed, they never knowingly broke a commandment. And yet there was in my father's character a stream of kindness running deeper than any behavior imposed by teaching nuns and parish priests, while my mother doled out her kindness only to those who deserved it. For nearly fifty years I had thought they were alike in their goodness, for her kindness had engulfed me like my father's, but now, for the first time, because of my remark on that summer afternoon, I saw the stream dry up.

Of course I apologized, but she was too deeply injured to forgive me. Of course I grieved over those next nine years—it was her intention that I should suffer—but she suffered more intensely than I. She couldn't get past the fact that her only child, her pride and joy, had told her to keep her nose out of his business. What was there to live for? The daybook in which she had been noting, throughout her life, the major events of our extended family, abruptly ends with these words written on that day: "What's the use of living?" What I had done amounted, in her mind, to matricide, and this together with my father's declining health cast her into a serious case of clinical depression that had her wishing for death herself. During the several days of watching at her deathbed, I was revising another novel, *Dear James,* so I had my writing to fall back on once again, my device for warding off grief. In this work is a character based primarily on my mother. Her name is Agatha McGee. She, too, is what I call "good by the book," doling out her kindnesses to those who deserve them and reprimanding those who don't. And yet in each episode, her heart is softened, her rigidity breaks down, love wins the day. I see this in retrospect as the feeble attempt of the novelist to move his mother in the same direction. From watching my mother suffer on principle through her final years, I learned the difference between a natural sort of friendliness and friendliness by the book. My father's spontaneous warmth was more attractive than my mother's rigorous goodness, but her rigor was still goodness nonetheless.

3

two elizabeths

Angel of Mercy

Grandmother Hassler was a pioneer. Grandfather Hassler, too, was a pioneer, but he looked to me like a man who had cracked under the strain, like someone who'd snuffed out his vital spark well before he died. I could be wrong, for I never got to know him well—he died when I was six—but I remember him as shriveled and ill. I picture him sitting in his black rocking chair by the oil stove in their small house in Perham, Minnesota, not rocking, but looking warily out from behind his mustache at a world that threatened or mystified him. His name was August. He wasn't the kind of grandfather you had fun with. People warned you not to jump onto his lap.

My grandmother's name was Elizabeth. In that small town in western Minnesota, she was the angel of mercy personified. She nursed the sick and dying. She served as midwife. She laid out the dead for burial. She went each day to the hospital and gathered up the bloody sheets and linens and took them home and washed them for a penny an item. "They called her Lizzie," I was once told by a cousin of hers, an old monk living in a monastery. "Anybody have an accident or come down sick, first thing they say, 'Go get Lizzie.'"

She was large, strong, and resourceful. Surely there was something of the servant or lackey in her that drew her readily out of a night's sleep at the first call from some townsman in trouble, no matter how distant his house or cold the night. She thought of herself as serving God.

There's no stinting, of course, when you're convinced you're doing God's work, and she had that unquestioning faith in God that we tend to believe was common to that generation, the sort of faith that allows you not only to know God but to know what road he wants you to take at all times.

Gradually her work dwindled. The hospital acquired a washing machine. A mortician moved to town. Her children grew up and contributed to her support. By the time I got well acquainted with her, she was very old and very large. She moved in with her daughter and son-in-law and suffered a long cancerous illness in their front parlor, where her bed had been moved from upstairs so that she was easier to tend to. She died the day I turned eighteen, in 1951. An autopsy revealed that much of her obesity was tumorous.

I have a photo of my grandmother standing on their front steps, looking very masculine despite her long voluminous skirts down to her shoetops. Studying the photo now, I see perseverance in her face, together with a look of happy contentment, and I see therefore where my father's doggedness and his everlasting good nature came from.

An Educated Aunt

Aunt Elizabeth was my mother's aunt. She began her teaching career in a one-room schoolhouse in rural Minnesota and finished up as the supervisor of elementary education in Montgomery County, Maryland. She was a stronger influence in my life than any of my grandparents, both because she outlasted them and because she lived with us from time to time.

The times were summers. She came to us to escape the heat of Washington, D.C., and to chatter and laugh with my mother just as Bunny had done a dozen years earlier. Except that my parents now owned a grocery store of their own, and clerking there was taking more and more of my mother's time, so I had Aunt Elizabeth to myself a good deal. My parents were superb parents and would have been sufficient to my future well-being, but along came bookish Aunt Elizabeth like an unexpected reward, and once again, as when Bunny came to live with us, the elders in my household formed a doting, beneficent tribunal. It's no wonder that I, an only child, grew up to feel at home in the world.

Professionally speaking, Aunt Elizabeth's achievements must have been one of the great success stories of her generation. Born the middle of nine children in the 1880s on a small farm near the village of Rose Creek, Minnesota, she probably knew no one with a college degree, except the parish priest, until she enrolled at the University of Minnesota to earn one of her own. After a few years of teaching in small towns of her home state, she went to New York and earned a master's in education at Columbia. So she, too, was a kind of pioneer.

Surely her accomplishments were greater than her family back on the farm could appreciate. But not so her wit. Or her family feeling. Or her joy. Everyone loved her for these traits. Hers was an intelligence spiced with just the right amount of wryness and skepticism to make her interesting—indeed, to make her essential to any family gathering. Haven't we all known someone who keeps the party from being a complete success by failing to be there? Or makes a house lonesome by being absent from it? Aunt Elizabeth was that person. Not that she was particularly ebullient. Her manner, in fact, was rather low-key, her expression deadpan, but whenever she told a story or passed a judgment or gave an order, there was a precision and a rightness about it—and a flash of humor about it—that somehow made life rich and fun and sensible.

Aunt Elizabeth was unlike Grandmother Elizabeth in more ways than merely her education and sophistication. Although she performed a thousand kindnesses for those she loved, Aunt Elizabeth was not, like my grandmother, submissive or servantlike. She was blunt and outspoken, though her thrusts were delivered with such wit that even if you were her target you were tempted to smile. And although a Catholic, she was not the blind follower of the parish priest that my grandmother was. In fact, she disliked the clergy as a group, but not as intensely as she disliked the Catholic sisterhood. Nuns, she used to say, were spoiled and lazy sissies.

No Happy Endings

Like lifelong teachers everywhere, Aunt Elizabeth's inner clock was set to school time, and even after she retired she continued to live in the East during the school term and to come to stay with us from June through Labor Day. I saw very little of her during the last five summers of her life because I was living some distance away with my wife and children. It's been said that there are no happy endings, and looking back over my sixty-eight years of life, I'm tempted to believe it, for a lot of my acquaintances who deserved good endings, in my opinion, didn't get them. My mother told me about the day Aunt Elizabeth was taken to the hospital after lunch with a vague feeling of illness and shortness of breath. Initially she was thought to be in no danger, and so my mother and father were sent home, and she was left alone and died of heart failure that very afternoon before anyone came to tend to her. When my parents got word and rushed to the hospital, they were stopped at her door by a doctor who advised them not to go in and see her. He didn't explain. He could only have meant that she had gone through some agonizing death struggle that left her unsightly.

How awful to think she had no one to help her through her last moments on earth. But that was her way, wasn't it? She alone of all her siblings left the farm for the university. She went to New York alone. She never married. In other words, she explored a lot of undiscovered territory by herself, and death, though as old as the human race, is the most undiscovered territory of all.

As dissimilar as these two Elizabeths appeared, I am struck by how they both went about their duties with holy zeal. The dissimilarity is primarily in the different levels of society in which they lived and worked. While my grandmother was toiling away at the foundations of life, where bedsheets become bloodstained from birth and death, my great-aunt was working upstairs in the library and sitting room, where we become civilized. These are social levels, not levels of greater or lesser worth. If the world had to choose between these two women, I suppose Aunt Elizabeth would prove dispensable, because before you can get on with living you have to have the bloody sheets washed and put away. But how grim life would be without that woman in the sitting room asking you to come up beside her on the couch so she can read you a story.

4

my irish grandfather

Poles Apart

My mother's parents, like my father's, seemed poles apart
in personality. Here they stand in my family photo album
in their backyard, at 4144 Aldrich Avenue South in
Minneapolis, posing for a snapshot. It is 1944 or '45. My
grandfather, whose name was Frank Callinan, is speaking
and scowling, perhaps offering gruff advice to the
photographer, while my grandmother, Mary, wears her
customary expression of fretfulness. What's worrying her
today? Her brother Tom's cancer? Her nephew missing in
action in Belgium? Did her dinner guests get enough to
eat? Mary Callinan was a very serious woman, perhaps a
bit less assertive than the typical Irish matriarch, but no
less puritanical, and known throughout all branches of the
family for her culinary skills. She was loved to the point of
idolatry by everyone, it seemed, but me.

As a child of course I didn't question her saintliness,
but I often wondered, and still do, what was so lovable
about her. She didn't exude warmth; she exuded worry.
There was a reserve about her, a kind of chilly stiffness
that may have inspired respect—but love? Ah, well, I have
to remind myself that generations of Catholics had been
surrounded at worship by the cold stone statues of saints
whom we had been trained to love as well.

The Old Conductor

Her husband, as far as I know, was the only true "character" ever to turn up in my ancestry. He was unfailingly

gregarious. He told stories to anyone who'd listen, and most often they were railroad stories, for Grandfather Callinan had been a conductor on the Milwaukee Road. Railroads were his abiding interest throughout his life. As he grew older, he told these stories with more and more immediacy, as if he'd just come in off his run between Austin, Minnesota, and Calmer, Iowa—as if he hadn't lost his job on his beloved Milwaukee Road as long ago as 1914. This I learned after his death in 1954. He'd been fired forty years earlier for letting his friends ride free of charge.

The year I turned six, Grandfather Callinan was seventy-three and reading to me, in its tedious entirety, *Jo's Boys* by Louisa May Alcott. About the book itself, I remember nothing except the engravings that turned up all too rarely on its pages, yet what I do remember is how eagerly I crawled onto his lap each evening for that lengthy session of drowsy pleasure, my ear pressed against his starched shirtfront, his lulling voice droning on and on, punctuated here and there by the clicking of his dentures and by the little whistles and wheezes emanating from his chest after a lifetime of pipe smoking.

And he took me to movies. Both of us were mightily moved by Dumbo's troubles in the circus, and we laughed ecstatically at the treeful of hard-bitten, cigar-smoking crows singing "When I See an Elephant Fly." I also recall the tears of joy that sprang into our eyes—as well as the eyes of James Cagney—when President

Roosevelt bestowed his blessing on George M. Cohan at the end of *Yankee Doodle Dandy.*

When I was thirteen and Grandfather was eighty, we journeyed together by rail to Oshkosh, Wisconsin, for a two-week vacation—from what?—at my uncle John's house on Lake Winnebago. The seats and aisles of the train were packed with soldiers in uniform on their way to Camp McCoy; some of the smaller men even lay sleeping in the overhead luggage racks. All those within earshot grew deferential toward Grandfather as he spun out his skein of railroad stories, pointing out the fact that we were traveling the very same roadbed he had traveled as a young conductor on the Milwaukee Road. At home I'd stopped listening to these stories, for he told them all over town and I'd heard each one about a million times, but now, sitting on my suitcase and seeing how they impressed the United States Army, I saw these stories in a fresh light once again. For the first time in a long while, I wasn't embarrassed whenever he paused, for the effect of heightening the drama, to light his pipe.

As a teenager, I was struck by the awkwardness of certain of my friends in the company of adults. The wider the age span the more difficult it was for them to look their elders in the eye and speak in words rather than in self-conscious grunts. Grandfather, by this time, was hard of hearing though still eager for conversation; they quite often didn't even acknowledge his presence, but glanced at him indifferently as though he were an

artifact under glass. I was puzzled by what I took to be
their general hostility toward adults—an attitude I didn't
share and couldn't understand. But of course it wasn't
hostility at all. It was that uncertainty we feel in the
presence of any wildly exotic creature. Yet to me, no
adult was completely unfamiliar, because in the process
of bridging the seventy-year gap between my grandfather
and me, I had somehow learned to bridge the lesser gaps
as well.

And how did I come to know this old man so well? By
means of stories. The endless stories he told me and the
stories we read together and watched on the screen were a
great education to me. His laughter and tears at Dumbo,
for example, might have been my textbook on human
empathy. And even before that, hadn't I delved to the core
of the old man when I listened with one ear to *Jo's Boys*
and kept the other ear pressed to his beating heart?

Stories endear us to one another. Time and time again
in my novels I find myself becoming more and more
sympathetic to a character as I spin out his or her story. I
can begin with a powerful dislike for someone like
Wallace Flint in *Grand Opening* or Imogene Kite in *Dear
James* and finish with a fresh understanding of the dis-
advantages that shaped them and a sympathy for their
eccentricities and flaws. And so it occurs to me now that
those who professed love for my Grandmother Callinan
simply understood her better than I did. Had I known
her story, I too might be singing her praises today.

But getting back to Grandfather, I have one more story to tell in which he proves to be more than merely a garrulous old storyteller. As an aimless freshman in college, majoring in business, I sought his aid in convincing my parents that my best career move might be to drop out and go to work for the Northern Pacific Railroad, where a number of my contemporaries were already earning the princely sum of three hundred dollars a month. Who better to enlist as my ally than the old conductor himself? Home for a weekend and preparing for bed in the room we shared, I therefore told Grandfather of my railroad ambitions. It took me a while to lay out my motives, and by the time I rested my case, the lights were out and the only sound from the next bed was the rattle of Grandfather's respiration. Had I talked him to sleep? Or had he, God forbid, turned off his hearing aid before I began? I rolled over and was nearly asleep when up through a fit of phlegmy throat-clearing and across the dark room came his voice:

"Only a damn fool would quit school to work on the railroad."

So I returned to campus, switched my major to English, and spent the rest of my enjoyable time there reading stories.

5

timmy and jackie

A Nine-Year-Old Terrorist

When, at the age of ten, I conspired to derail a train, I felt little if any guilt, because I was merely following directions. That the director, Timmy Musser, was only nine years old and probably not of sound mind, apparently made no difference to me. My parents, as well as the nuns who'd been my teachers for four years, having instilled in me a sharp sense of obedience, had stopped short of discernment, and so here I was, a fifth grader and the new boy in town (we had recently moved to Plainview, Minnesota), willingly joining Timmy as his stupidly obedient henchman.

All four Mussers, who lived across the street from us and next door to the stockyards, were given to what struck me as odd behavior. Mrs. Musser preserved meat the way I had seen my mother put up peaches and tomatoes, in jars to store in the cellar. Furthermore, she probably suffered from agoraphobia, leaving the confines of her house and yard only once a week, scurrying off to St. Joachim's Church before the Sunday morning sun was up to attend six o'clock Mass. Mr. Musser, unlike my own father, never lifted a finger to help around the house—and a tiny house it was, with its back door pushed up against the gigantic oil drums beside the railroad embankment. Evenings Mr. Musser divested himself of his work clothes down to his socks, pants, and suspenders and took his ease on the couch, ignoring the loose door hinges and cracked windowpanes while he droned on and on about his job at the nearby Lakeside Packing Company. His wife, busily darning socks or knitting, appeared to be listening to him, but no one else did. Not I, who lay on the floor with Timmy, trying to teach him the game of checkers; not Timmy, whose conniving, criminal mind had no room in it for games or make-believe or whimsy of any sort; not Lou, his older sister, a Latin beauty who busied herself with her high-school homework under the dim and only lamp in the room.

Lou's odd behavior was tied up with her holiness. She never went out with boys or read magazines, her mother told me proudly, and she saw only religious movies, such as *The Song of Bernadette*. What's more, she went to confession every week. Lou was preparing herself to follow in the footsteps of an older sister and become (in Timmy's words) "a goddam nun out in California."

If God was leading Lou into the convent, then surely Satan had prison in mind for Timmy. Already as a fourth grader, Timmy Musser had the instincts of a hardened gangster. He wore on his round little face an unchanging expression of great seriousness, and by the unceasing movement of his eyes—deliberate rather than shifty—he seemed always to be planning his next heist or some other act of mayhem while checking to see if he was being followed.

(And what place, my reader is asking, does Timmy the Terrorist have in a book on goodness? Why are we wasting time with this miscreant? He's here, first, because goodness shines brighter when held up against its opposite; second, because in taking stock of myself, in finding my place on the good-and-evil continuum, I need to see the two extremes; and third, because although he moved away before he was ten and I never saw or heard of him again, Timmy, to this day, strikes me as such a fascinating creature.)

The day of our attempted derailment, a Saturday in late August, began with Timmy stealing, from the back of a pickup truck idling at the stockyards gate, an enormous steel crowbar and hiding it in the weeds beneath the oil drums.

"Why?" I asked in my innocence.

"We'll need it to tip over the train this afternoon," he said.

The train in question was a freight, usually not more than three cars long, that came to town six days a week in summer, less often when the packing plant was shut down, in order to haul canned vegetables to market, as well as livestock from the stockyards and grain from the elevator at the center of town. An odd thing about this train was that because Plainview was its terminus and yet had no turntable, it arrived front first and left town backwards. It usually arrived around two o'clock, and by two-thirty of this Saturday afternoon, Timmy was pouting and cursing under his breath. The train, it seemed, had already cut out its Saturday run, and because next week school would start, we wouldn't have another chance until mid–October, when the faculty gave us two days off while they attended their convention. "Well, we'll make up for it then, goddammit," said Timmy. "We'll derail two trains."

Then, in the distance, the whistle of the locomotive sounded, and Timmy's face underwent an immediate transformation. I read not only joy but perfect peace in his eyes. And when the train rounded a curve and came in sight beyond the stockyards, his smile intensified to laughter. Hidden high among the oil drums by this time, we watched the engine with its coal tender uncouple itself from the three cars and caboose and back onto the spur behind the warehouse of Lakeside Packing, where it hooked up to a waiting boxcar and then reattached itself to the rest of the train. It stopped next at the stockyards where it took a couple of men nearly half an hour to drive a bunch of yelping, elusive pigs up a chute and into a cattle car. Now Timmy grew tense, waiting to see if the train would come further into town or go back where it came from. It advanced, chugged below us, and rounded a curve to the grain elevator. As soon as it was out of sight, we scampered down to ground level, and I watched for traffic at the crossing while Timmy inserted the crowbar in a switch. He'd tried this before, he told me. He'd wedged a two-by-six piece of lumber into the switch well before the train arrived, but the engineer saw it and stopped and the fireman climbed down out of the locomotive and kicked it away, assuming (Timmy presumed) that it was a piece of construction debris.

We scrambled back up to our perch. This being the highest point of land for miles around, I could see the bell towers of the two biggest churches in town, St. Joachim's Catholic and Immanuel Lutheran, standing as sentinels of the soul at opposite ends of Main Street. I could see the roof of our store, where my parents were at work, and I wished I were there instead of shivering in the wind atop this rusty oil drum waiting to see a disaster I'd helped bring about.

Timmy, suddenly alert to the distant dingdong of the bell and the chuffing of steam, said, "Damn it to hell" and pointed down at the switch. The crowbar, worn shiny from use as a tire iron, was glistening brightly in the sun. "They'll see it, goddammit, they'll see it."

"No they won't," said I, earnestly hoping they would. Now, with the train backing lazily around the bend, I was terrified. Someone would die. We would be caught and put in prison.

On chugged the train, neither slowing down nor speeding up. "Damn them fartblossoms," seethed Timmy, "they ain't goin' fast enough to tip over."

With my heart in my throat, I watched the caboose hit the switch and teeter. Fearful as I was, I felt triumphant as well, inasmuch as the scene below proved that one could work one's will on the world. It only required that you were calculating enough beforehand and sneaky enough to carry it out. Choosing a weaker victim was essential of course, the way this fourth-grade prodigy at my side had chosen a mere railroad train and its crew.

The caboose didn't tip over or slide off the rails. It stopped, still rocking, and the brakeman stepped out on the back platform and looked every direction but up. The engineer and the fireman came running.

"We'd better go," I said, shrinking back from the edge of the oil drum we lay upon.

Without taking his eyes from the tracks, Timmy asked why.

"We'll get caught," said I, finding with my foot the top rung of the ladder.

I understood why Timmy wanted to stay. What was the good of an act of violence if you weren't around to study the consequences? But I'll never understand where he got the courage to do so, to keep poking his head over the edge to take it all in, right up to the point when the crew climbed aboard and the rest of the train drew slowly across the switch and then, with a triumphant toot and dingdong, chugged off between the fields of corn. I wasn't there for that part. I was listening from the safety of the Mussers' kitchen, where, dripping with the sweat of fear and panting with relief, I was watching Timmy's beautiful and saintly sister help the reclusive Mrs. Musser stuff handfuls of cooked beef into glass jars.

A Twelve-Year-Old Saint

Within a month of our arrival in Plainview, and completely untutored, I began serving Mass at St. Joachim's. This being a nunless parish and its old and ascetic pastor, Father O'Connor, being too far removed from the mundane to bother instructing a mere child of ten, I apprenticed myself to the only experienced server in the parish, a boy named Jackie.

Jackie was the good-natured son of a widow who cleaned houses for a living. He was two years older than I and the object of my great admiration, not only because he was a faultless altar boy—dedicated, devout, punctual, and obedient—but also because he seemed smarter than a lot of Catholics I knew, and he had a wry sense of humor. At this point in my life, it seemed to me that I had met, among the truly religious, an overabundance of humorless types, and I'd begun to suspect that stodginess and slowness of mind might be a prerequisite to holiness. Jackie disabused me of this line of thought. Whenever Father O'Connor lost his way in the pulpit and followed an irrelevant path into private peeves and musings, Jackie, sitting beside me in the sanctuary, would turn his wise little grin in my direction as if to say, "How pathetic" and hope, I'm sure, for an answering grin from me.

Outside of church, however, we saw very little of each other—such is the gap between a fifth grader and a seventh grader—and yet, when at the end of our first year in Plainview we moved from the stockyards neighborhood to the opposite end of town, I found myself living just a few doors down the block from Jackie. I imagined that somehow, despite the difference in our ages, we might become friends; but it was too late for that. By this time, Jackie was dying.

I was perhaps his only regular visitor. I went every Saturday after lunch. His mother had converted the front room of their small house into Jackie's bedroom so that he could watch the passing traffic on Highway 42 from his bed. What did we do or say during my visits? We may have played a hand or two of rummy, and maybe we looked over the assignments I brought him from his homeroom teacher, but I have no memory of anything but inconsequential small talk. It's a characteristic of anyone growing up in a happy household, I've found, this ability to wring every possible remark out of an unremarkable topic. Around people we're fond of, our urge to converse is far greater than our need to do so, and we therefore talk at length about little, stringing out our words the way spiders emit the filament of their webs. Then, too, imitating my parents in the store, I was growing proficient at small talk, particularly with old people, and Jackie was about as old as he was going to get.

At first I had gone to see him under orders from my mother. Visiting the sick was a corporal work of mercy, after all, and she was eager for me to start building up some credit in eternity—and at no risk, for rheumatic fever, unlike polio, was noncontagious. But soon I found myself making these visits of my own accord, for I was finding more and more about Jackie to be fond of—and curious about. "This seeing the sick endears them to us," says Gerard Manley Hopkins, which of course is true, but as compelling as my fellow feeling was my curiosity about the spiritual change worked upon him by his weakening heart. He was going through the same shrinking stages we witness now and then in a public figure who will allow himself to waste away on the television news—Hubert Humphrey twenty years ago, more recently Cardinal Bernardin of Chicago—but I'm not talking about his outward transformation so much as a change from within. His illness seemed to relax him, seemed to purify him, seemed to lend him a kind of transparency through which I could see quite plainly the sweetness of his soul.

One sunny day in late autumn, for example, gazing out the window, Jackie's eyes settled on the distant athletic field and he remarked, "I can see you guys playing football over there after school." He said this without a trace of envy in his voice, with no hint of anguish or despair. Whereas I, with my obsessive love of football, would doubtless have been bitterly frustrated in his place, Jackie seemed to be speaking out of sheer pleasure.

Or again: his older sister's husband, dismayed by Jackie's loss of weight, stopped in with a quart of ice cream one Saturday and demanded that he eat all of it nonstop. This was shortly before my arrival, and when I arrived I found Jackie bloated and amused as he slowly spooned up the last of the ice cream. His brother-in-law stood over him looking smugly full of himself, believing, I suppose, that he'd just discovered the cure for rheumatic fever. And Jackie's sublime smile said that he believed it too, but of course this was for his brother-in-law's benefit only, for when he turned to look at me I saw a flicker of the old wryness in his eyes. "We'll put some meat on that kid's bones yet," the brother-in-law explained to me on his way out. "I'm coming back tomorrow with another quart." With his savior safely out of the way, Jackie asked me to bring him the basin from the drainboard in the kitchen, then he asked me to please go outside and come back later. Leaving, I heard him begin to vomit.

God knows how many quarts of ice cream Jackie forced down and brought up again to sustain his family's hope. I know only that the more I saw of Jackie's self-abnegation, the more fascinating it became. Wasn't this the sort of God-pleasing humility the church had been urging on me since the first grade? But with this difference: Jackie wasn't being humble for God's sake, or the church's, or even his brother-in-law's; he was being simply himself.

Here then was virtue in its pure form, and I found it every bit as attractive as Timmy Musser's evil bent. I longed to be as good as Jackie, and yet, at the tender age of eleven and twelve I somehow knew that to reach his level of virtue, I would need to drop my pride, my self-regard, the very idea that I was being virtuous. I was much too self-aware to be as good as Jackie. Or as bad as Timmy, for that matter. For isn't it this same lack of self-regard that allows the thief, the terrorist, the train-derailer to carry out his mischief? So I would never be a candidate for either sainthood or prison. With my proclivity for patient watchfulness, I would always play the role of the idle bystander. I could thrill to tales of derring-do, and I could admire sainthood, but I'd never come close to either end of the morality scale. My place was at the intersection, watching for traffic while the crowbar was inserted in the switch. My place was in the chair beside the deathbed.

I made one last trip to Jackie's house, this time on a spring evening, with my parents, to view his body. We found the kitchen crowded with Jackie's brothers (one wearing a Navy uniform) and sister and their families. Jackie, in his coffin, had the front room practically to himself, while we the living ate his mother's homemade cookies and made cheery small talk. We were reluctant to leave each other's company for more than the few seconds it took to step through the open doorway and mumble a prayer over the body. I didn't even do that. I, who had given him part of every Saturday for almost a year, had no time for him now.

It was a dark rainy morning when most of the eighth grade and I from the sixth were released from class and hurried down the street to St. Joachim's, where I put on my black requiem cassock and my white surplice, and then, bearing the crucifix on a staff, I led Father O'Connor and the coffin and the drenched mourners into the crowded church as the organ and choir broke out in their loud lament, which was made to seem even graver than usual, more sorrowful, by the undertone of rain pounding relentlessly on the roof.

And yet I didn't feel the sting of Jackie's death during his funeral Mass. I was too full of myself as an altar boy, imagining how I must look to my schoolmates, particularly the Protestants and the nonchurchgoers. How admirably I went about my duties on the altar. How amazing and mysterious were the phrases I cried out in sharp contrast to Father O'Connor's mumbled prayers. "Dominuuuu vobiscuuuu," droned the priest. "ET CUM SPIRITU TUO!" shouted I, twelve years old and St. Joachim's lone surviving altar boy.

At the cemetery a mile north of town, we discovered rainwater standing in the grave; small mudslides were coming loose around its perimeter. Although nobody mentioned it afterward, there must have been others besides me who were secretly horrified to think of lowering Jackie into eight or ten inches of chill water. When the priest finally finished recommending Jackie to God and closed his wet book, I handed him the sprinkler and he mixed a couple of shakes of holy water with the heavy raindrops thumping on the coffin lid. Then I

Timmy and Jackie

handed him the censer, and when he waved it in the direction of the grave as though it still held fire, a mighty gust of wind swept the cemetery with a fresh squall of horizontal rain, driving most of the mourners back to their cars. The undertaker, with the help of Jackie's brother and brothers-in-law—no time for decorum now—dropped the coffin into the grave, and that's when I was struck by the finality of Jackie's death, when the coffin hit bottom with a splash.

6

a scattering
of graces

One Night's Lodging

I have a friend named Nithy, an ambitious and great-hearted young man from Malaysia, who, with a companion of his, took it upon himself to ride his bicycle from the tip of South America to Minnesota. Despite his estimate that it would take them six months to travel these thousands of miles, they took along only enough money to pay for about fifteen nights' lodging. To take more, he insisted, would negate the purpose of the trip, which was to prove the brotherhood and sisterhood of most of humankind. Believing as he does in the intrinsic kindness of human nature, he would trust people they met along the way to put them up nights. So they flew to Argentina and began their trip with the back wheels of their bicycles in the waters off the coast of Tierra del Fuego, and when—211 days later—they arrived at their destination I asked Nithy how many nights he'd had to pay for a bed.

His answer was "One."

Now this is inspiring in itself, but among the many tales Nithy brought home from his adventure was one about the evening they were riding along an uninhabited stretch of road in Honduras, at the end of which, he discovered later, was a party of cutthroats lying in wait for just such unsuspecting innocents as these two young men on bicycles. It was growing dark when suddenly a car appeared beside them, driven by a woman they had never seen before, who told them that danger lay ahead and they must turn around. She herself turned around and drove off in the direction she'd come from, and they did likewise. They never saw the woman again.

This is the sort of occurrence that, if you put it in a work of fiction, would invalidate the entire piece because it is coincidental, too pat to be believed. And yet these things happen in life. People turn up to guide us, to lend us a helping hand, to cheer us on, and then they drop away. It's their precise timing that makes them seem like graces, sent by divine intervention. Scattered through my sixty-eight years have been a number of such people, intervening in my life at exactly the moment I needed them.

A Skill That Can't Be Taught

I came across my first inspiring teacher in college. I realize this is late; most people recall at least a few outstanding teachers from their elementary or high-school days. Perhaps there were such teachers in my early classrooms too, but I, being a bored and mediocre student at best, wasn't receptive to them. But then as a college freshman, like a good many of my contemporaries at St. John's, I was captivated by Steven B. Humphrey, professor of English.

It's difficult to say where his talent as a teacher lay. He was a short, unimposing figure with a strange habit of bending his head forward and turning it left and right, as though he had neck cramps. His magic may have been in his small yet wonderfully evocative voice as he read passages aloud from the books he assigned. Or perhaps in his searching eyes and the probing intelligence with which he led discussions. Or perhaps it was simply that he was the first person, and one of very few people, I've ever known whose life was devoted entirely to literature.

Without Steve Humphrey's example, I wonder if I would have come to understand what a faithful, lifelong companion literature can be. My parents had started me out very early as a reader, but while they both continued to read for the rest of their lives, their main business wasn't with books. Like everyone I knew as a boy, they were busy about other things. Even my high-school English teachers, I have to admit with shame, devoted much more time and energy to controlling their unruly students than to the pleasures of literature.

But here was a man, a bachelor living in a dormitory, who seemed to be sustained through life by the books surrounding him on his floor-to-ceiling shelves. He was one of those laymen you will sometimes find living in the shadow of a monastery, outdoing the monks in their dedication to their vocation. Steve Humphrey's vocation was not only teaching college English, but for me, teaching—by example—how to teach.

Victory by Joseph Conrad was the first novel he assigned his freshmen. I found it difficult reading and so looked eagerly forward to class each day, where he made perfect sense of the story while pointing out the author's most impressive passages. As a senior, I took three more of his classes: Contemporary Drama, Contemporary Fiction, and Methods of Teaching English. It was in his fiction class that I gained an immediate fondness for the likes of Hemingway, Fitzgerald, and Graham Greene and developed a lifelong hunger to know what the latest of my contemporaries is writing.

There were only six or eight of us heading out to be high-school English teachers and thus required to take Methods of Teaching English. I'm not aware of a single method taught in this class—we spent the semester diagramming sentences on the board. Not that it mattered. Teaching, I believe, is a skill that can't be taught. What I took away from this class was Steve's example of making every subject—even the diagramming of sentences—interesting. From this good and dedicated man, I learned a style of teaching that served me well during my long career in the classroom. I imitated his manner of reading aloud, of looking my students in the eye, and of using conversation, instead of the lecture, as the primary means of arriving at an appreciation of literature. Whether I succeeded in these areas, I have no idea. I do know, however, that I have come close to him in my dedication to good literature. He topped off my education as a reader, taking my interest in literature, which dated back to my early childhood, and shaping it into a vital and lasting companionship.

And I went one step beyond Steve Humphrey, particularly during my early years as a high-school teacher.

When I discovered how much students of that age enjoyed them, I told them tales from my personal life. As a college student studying this paragon, I had often wondered if Steve Humphrey felt passion for anything besides literature. In other words, what did his personal life amount to? Not much, I discovered twenty-five years later when I returned to St. John's to join him in the English department. During one particular term, when he was on vacation, I moved into his apartment and served as his substitute proctor in the dormitory. One day, searching through his desk for a pencil, I came across a half sheet of paper containing a list, with the words "Chronicle of My Life" written at the top. Who could resist reading such a list? Not I. But what a disappointment. It was a list of medical problems and procedures—a siege of pneumonia, a gallbladder operation, a sinus infection, each precisely dated in chronological order—and nothing else.

Ma Taylor

I don't remember her first name, if I ever knew it. She was Mrs. Taylor to the student body and Ma Taylor to those on the faculty who were amused by her autocratic ways. She was a stylish woman who had a queenly bearing about her. She and I arrived in the tiny town of Fosston in northwestern Minnesota in the fall of 1956, she to finish out her last two or three years before retirement as our high-school librarian and I—my second year out of college—to teach English across the hall from the library and, come spring, to direct the senior class play.

Finding the library a terrible mess, Mrs. Taylor's first act was to close it for the month of September while she organized the card catalogue and all the miscatalogued books. Then, open for business, she ruled over the library as if it were her home, inquiring of all who entered their reason for being there and demanding perfect order and silence from students who, like mine, were forced into the library from time to time by their teachers.

In the spring the class play I directed was a courtroom drama called *The People vs. Maxine Lowe.* I remember very little about the plot except that Maxine Lowe, on trial for murder, was not the main character. The two opposing attorneys, played by two of my better students, were on stage almost constantly and had to learn so many lines that I concentrated all my attention on them and pretty much ignored the parade of witnesses called to testify, whose portrayals were scarcely adequate. At one of our last rehearsals, at which I was greatly relieved to find that everyone had memorized his or her lines and was ready, I thought, for opening night, I saw Mrs. Taylor watching from the shadows at the rear of the auditorium. Her presence there forced me to look at the production through the eyes of an audience, and I saw that it had no vigor, no color, no pizzazz. Well, I wasn't working with professionals, after all. My cast was a bunch of rural high-school kids getting up and speaking by rote.

Twenty-four hours later, at dress rehearsal, I was surprised and even excited by a spirited vigor that seemed infectious among the players. They came onstage with confidence, and several of them, dressed in costumes I hadn't thought to assign them, gave convincing performances. Maxine Lowe in particular came onstage looking positively exotic, wearing bright red lipstick and a wide-brimmed green and gauzy hat.

The next night, with the auditorium nearly filled with friends and relatives of the large cast for our one and only performance, my players outdid themselves. Maxine Lowe, in addressing the prosecuting attorney, had even developed a sassy tone I hadn't thought to advise her about. The audience was very pleased, and so was I. What a fine bunch of natural actors, I thought—until the end, when I congratulated Maxine on her performance, her costume, her makeup.

"Oh, it isn't my doing," she said. "Thank Mrs. Taylor. She's been working with us yesterday and today in the library, teaching us how to act."

Taming the Savages

At the time in my family life when things were beginning to spin out of control, when our children were very small and needed more stability than my first wife or I could give them—I'm talking about 1960—we changed our place of residence in the town where I was teaching high-school English. On the very first day in our new location, our three children found their way across the alley and into the welcoming arms of the Wickstroms.

"Wick" Wickstrom was a sixty-year-old lineman for the REA, the Rural Electrification Association, which brought power and light to the people outside the city limits. Due to a weak heart, Wick's pole-climbing days were behind him, but he went out every day as foreman of the line crew, for he knew the location and condition of every electrical line in the 2,400 square miles covered by the association. And more important, he was acquainted with the entire population of that area, no matter how far back in the woods their houses were tucked. Now, it's a fact of life that a certain percentage of remote-living people are insecure rednecks who will challenge anyone crossing their property line. Sometimes, parking near such places, the crew wouldn't get out of their trucks until Wick, with his affable, nonthreatening nature, went in and tamed these "jack-pine savages," as he called them.

Wick was one of the most amusing and graphic story-tellers I've ever met. Across forty years I can still hear him describe with a chuckle the film of honey spread across the kitchen table of one such redneck family who invited him in for coffee, and when he got up to leave he couldn't raise his elbows off the table.

It was easy to see why children took to Wick. His was a smiling, friendly nature. Anne Wickstrom, on the other hand, was a stern-looking, stern-talking woman, and yet my children sensed the good heart under her gruff facade and loved her like a grandmother from the start. Most likely her charm lay in the food she served the moment any guest walked through the door. I can still taste her delicious raisin cake with butterscotch frosting.

Whimsical Roots

A strong bond develops among people facing adversity together. Between 1965 and 1968, this sort of bond was formed among seven of us untenured instructors at Bemidji State College (now University), which is located deep in the woods of northern Minnesota. In my novel *Rookery Blues* there is a short passage, perhaps unfair, that portrays Bemidji State as I thought of it in those years: "A campus was a kind of asylum where professors diverted themselves year after year with academic questions. . . . Which student should be spared an F as too demeaning? Which colleague should be denied tenure as too ennobling? How big a budget for hockey sticks?"

Having been recruited by the BSC English department after ten exhausting years of high-school teaching, I knew at once that I had found my academic niche. Not only did I discover myself on the same wavelength with college students, but now at last I had ample time to correct papers and prepare for class. And yet, being a talented classroom teacher wasn't good enough. The adversity I speak of was the threat of dismissal that was held over us unless we earned our doctor's degrees.

To start with, there were four of us insecure young men in the humanities division who gravitated into each other's company—Dick, Jim, Irv, and me. Jim, in the English department, was the youngest scholar, having come to Bemidji with a fresh master's degree from St. Louis University. Irv, the son of a Lutheran minister from North Dakota, had given up on a doctoral program at a large Midwestern university; he taught Russian. Dick, a teacher of French, was a duck hunter who had come, like I had, from a high-school faculty in the midst of the Mississippi waterfowl flyway, and although ducks were less plentiful around Bemidji, he and I spent a good many sunrises sitting in blinds together, sipping coffee and hoping to see something to shoot at.

At first it was ice fishing that formed the bond among the four of us. Several Saturdays during our first winter in Bemidji, the four of us drove an hour farther north to Red Lake and brought home our limit of walleyes. Then as the tenuousness of our jobs became ever more obvious, we began to hold meetings of our own—mock meetings—usually in a bar, where we drank a lot of brandy and turned college policy on its head, praising academic failure and condemning academic success. We called ourselves The Scholars.

During our second year of existence, we four named ourselves the Founding Fathers when three more of the faculty—Don, Ray, and John—applied for, and were granted, admission. All three of them, about ten years older than us four founders, were forever after referred to as "Junior Members." It was either a tribute to our gregarious fun or due to the misery of teaching in such a remote, snowbound location that two of these junior members already held doctor's degrees and were about to become tenured, while the third, Don, was at work on his.

With time, The Scholars as an entity became more bureaucratic and its meetings more ritualized. For example, Irv, after serving as our first president, was appointed keeper of the carpet, which meant that he showed up at each of our quarterly meetings with a small swatch of a blue carpet hanging from a rope around his neck, and this he would place on the floor for a member to stand on while being called on the carpet for some bookish sort of success. I recall Dick standing humbly on the square of carpet and being soundly castigated for returning from the University of Missouri with his doctorate.

As with any organization, we were pulled in several directions at the whim of the members. When a president, such as myself, became dictatorial, John, who'd been appointed our prince of whimsy, would call us back to our whimsical roots. When Junior Member Ray, never an enthusiastic fisherman, suggested we dispense with the annual December trip to Red Lake, he was overruled—until, approaching the age of fifty, even the Founding Fathers lost their enthusiasm for standing out in the wintry wind and staring at a watery hole in a vast sheet of ice.

In retrospect I see that if I had tried to stick it out at Bemidji State, though I had no intention of pursuing a doctor's degree, I may have been able to retain my job. Don and Irv, like me, lack the degree to this day, and they finished out their careers there, as did Dick, John, and Ray. For reasons of security, however, Jim and I found positions a hundred miles south at Brainerd Community College, and for ten years after we moved, the Bemidji delegation and the Brainerd delegation continued to meet in one venue or the other, or halfway between. Then, in 1980, when I moved a farther seventy miles to St. John's, The Scholars more or less disbanded.

But what a godsend they were. I never think back to those early uncertain years of my college teaching career without being grateful for the consoling, high spirited friendship of those six men. I hadn't surrounded myself with a group of friends like that since I was a boy in Plainview.

7

sacred places

Troops of Friends

Picture a village in the rich, rolling countryside of south-
eastern Minnesota, surrounded by fields of corn and cattle.
That was Plainview when I, at the age of ten, moved
there with my mother and father in 1943. It's still
Plainview in 2001—its population doubled to something
more than three thousand, the hilly fields planted in
contours instead of squares, a single supermarket having
taken the place of its six small grocery stores, but still a
town sustained by agriculture.

The farmers now are the grandsons and granddaughters
of those who crowded into town on Saturday evenings
in summer and listened to the weekly band concert,
took in the weekend Western at the Gem Theater,
bought a sack of popcorn at the popper in front of
Erding's Barbershop, watched a card game at Kruger's
Pool Hall, ate a meal at Timm's Cafe, and finally, near
midnight and like an afterthought, packed themselves
into the markets, including my parents' Red Owl Store,
for their week's supply of groceries.

We had come to this town from the north, by way of
my mother's native Minneapolis, where we'd spent some
months living, as we had during my infancy, with her
parents. My father and I much preferred the small town
to the city—his business thrived and I acquired troops of
friends—but my mother never got used to Plainview's
insular ways, never felt at home among a population
top-heavy with elderly retired farmers, never felt

appreciated by the superintendent of the schools where
she taught and served as part-time librarian.

For a long time I was happily oblivious to the
strong current of religious animosity running under
the surface of daily life in Plainview. How silly we
must have looked to the smaller congregations—the
Congregationalists, the Methodists, the Church of
Christers—we Catholics and Lutherans, competing for
power on the village council, trying to outvote one
another in school-board elections, patronizing only
those merchants whose theology matched our own,
and burying our dead in cemeteries a mile apart. The
mind-bending damage must have been done generations
before our arrival in town, for not once did I hear our
infirm and inward-looking old priest condemn Luther
or Lutheranism, nor did the Lutheran pastor, to the
best of my knowledge, disapprove of my friendship
with his son Donald.

It was the school-board election of 1949 or '50 that
brought the religious feuding to my attention. In my
novel *Grand Opening,* it's Brendan's mother who is
defeated in this election, whereas in actual fact it was my
father, but the method was the same in both cases. After
serving two productive terms on the board, my father
was drubbed by an uprising of Lutherans who'd apparently
decided that four years of service to the community was
enough for any papist. A secret phone campaign brought
out a surge of eleventh-hour Lutherans whose write-in

votes for their surprise candidate amounted to several more than my father's votes.

This experience loosened Plainview's hold on my father, who until then, happily busy in his store, had helped me resist my mother's desire to go back and live among the circle of friends she missed so sorely in the northern town we'd come from. And so, within three days of my graduation from high school, the local drayman, a Catholic by marriage, backed his ecumenical truck up to our door, and he and his Lutheran assistant went to work loading it with our furniture.

Because of this rather abrupt departure—and because Plainview had been the setting of my happy teenage years—I came to idealize this village in my memory. Thirty-five years after leaving town, in a novel based on our Plainview experience, I would make much of such things as the religious bigotry and other problematic elements of small-town life. Of course, tragedy is much more dramatic than happy endings, but I suspect I had another, less conscious motive. I must not have trusted the idyllic picture I'd been carrying around in my head all those years, and so I felt obliged to compensate for it by portraying the dark side of things. Surely Brendan Foster, my counterpart in the novel, does come of age in the story, as I did, and does learn important lessons about society and his place in it, as I did, but I've conveyed very little of the happiness that I myself experienced during the eight years of our residence there.

In that innocent time, before drugs, before television, small-town America was a wonderful place to grow up. Moving there from the city, I happened to join a fifth-grade class with a disproportionate number of athletic boys and immediately fell in love with sports. Having come from a school where the only game known to the teachers was pump-pump-pullaway, I was overjoyed, midmorning and midafternoon in grades five and six, at our being released from the classroom for twenty minutes of supervised athletics, usually kickball. I remember how shocked I was during the first of these recesses when my classmates, invoking the infield fly rule, challenged our teacher Mrs. Lance, who served as kickball umpire (surely no one at my previous school had ever heard of such a rule, much less dared to contradict the judgment of a teacher), and how astonished I was when she reversed her decision. I remember how my heart fell each day when I saw Mrs. Lance look at her watch and raise her whistle to her lips to call us back to the tedium of scholarship.

Outside of school hours, my friends and I plunged ourselves into pleasures unheard of in the city. In the cold, waning daylight we played football in the knee-deep snow. Evenings we packed ourselves into the high-decibel, crackerbox gymnasia of the Whitewater League, where we watched the high drama of the Plainview Gophers taking on basketball foes from St. Charles, Wabasha, Eyota, and Pine Island. By halftime of my first game, I knew each Gopher by name, because he was a friend's older brother, or at least the friend of a friend's older brother. When trout season opened in early April, we bicycled miles beyond the village limits with our fishing poles and pup tents and camped overnight in the bluffs along the Whitewater River.

Eventually I came to know the ecstasy of high-school football and, along with it, the pleasure of playing in almost perfect unison with one's fellow players, for by this time my friends—Babe, Don, Porky, Turk, Edwin, Pat, Gordy, Gene—and I had become part of a very good team. My specialty was tackling. I didn't have the strength of leg to be a running back, or enough bulk to be a lineman, but I did have the speed and fearlessness of a linebacker. In my maroon and gold uniform, number 38, I went up against the ballcarriers from Lewiston, Wabasha, Lake City, Stewartville, Cannon Falls, Dodge Center, and our archrival, St. Charles—and I knocked every one of them off his pins. Twenty-seven years later, when the first bound copy of my first novel arrived in the mail, I felt a thrill not unprecedented in my life. It was a thrill as great as, but no greater than, the sensation I felt the night in October 1950 that we beat St. Charles 49–0 on our way to the Whitewater League championship.

Getting Around to the Carrots

My association with St. John's University (in Collegeville, Minnesota) goes back a long way. I first laid eyes on the campus in the spring of 1950, when my parents and I attended the graduation of a cousin of mine. I liked the place a lot better on that spring afternoon than I did the next year as a student there. In those days freshmen were put through a pretty severe process of hazing, which entailed being ceremoniously beaten with paddles, wearing a humiliating green beanie for seven weeks, and having to serve as flunkies for upperclassmen. Then, too, I had enrolled as a business major and was getting poor grades in accounting. In my sophomore year, freed from the hazing and having changed my major to English, I was finally able to appreciate St. John's.

There's a unique constancy about the place, which emanates from St. John's Abbey. When I returned to campus as a teacher after twenty-five years away, the same men were still living there; many of them had been my professors, and some I had corresponded with over the years. It was like coming home. By the time of my retirement seventeen years later, I had followed the coffins of these old friends, one by one, out to the cemetery on the hill overlooking the lake. All but Father Godfrey, Father Vincent, and Father Virgil, that is.

Father Godfrey, the well-known liturgical reformer of Vatican II, has been ready to die for a very long time. Preparing to spend a semester in Israel, he predicted that he would die over there, in his Savior's native land. That was at least fifteen years ago. Last fall, meeting me on campus one day, he pointed to his carotid artery, which he said was 90 percent blocked and inoperable, claiming happily that God would be inviting him to his heavenly banquet within a few days. God, however, appears to be neglecting his guest list, for practically every publication coming out of St. John's these days has a photo of Godfrey enjoying yet another earthly banquet with some visiting dignitary.

Father Vincent, professor of history, appears determined to outlive it. Now in his late eighties, he is as vigorous and energetic as in the days fifty years ago when he led us through the history of Europe in our junior year, all of his lectures delivered with a curious little smile and punctuated with bursts of nervous laughter, making the story of humankind seem a kind of joke. Until exam time. I don't remember anyone else giving more difficult tests than Father Vincent. Having retired from the classroom decades ago, he was put in charge of the abbey archives, where he's been soaking up trivia ever since. At the recent funeral for one of his confreres, who was killed in a highway accident, Vincent brushed past me on the way to the open grave, saying with his inscrutable smile, "He was the first monk of our abbey to die in an automobile."

Father Virgil is another monk who, like Father Vincent, remains ageless into his eighties. I believe it's Virgil's twisted sense of humor that's keeping him alive. Nearly fifty years ago, in his Old Testament class, we came to the episode in which David, enamored with Bathsheba, sends Uriah off to war and hopes he'll be killed. Virgil said, "That's what the abbot did to

Mr. M——, you know." (Mr. M——, a layman on the faculty, was proving troublesome to the administration.)
"Father Abbot sent him off to World War II, hoping he
wouldn't come back, and then he told all of us monks at
the next chapter meeting, 'May his blood be upon us and
upon our children.'" I've repeated this story to Father
Virgil at least a half-dozen times over the last decade, and
he always denies having said any such thing, while laughing
out loud. Just last week Father Virgil inquired about my
health, particularly my Parkinson's, and I told him I'd
begun falling down fairly often. Most people react to this
news with alarm, but not Father Virgil. "Oh, that's good,"
he said in his refreshingly zany manner. "Falling down is
good for the heart."

Of the monks who've departed this life, I remember
especially Father Dunstan. What a gentleman. He was the
first professor I met when I enrolled in 1951, for he
happened to be at the table where I registered. He
suggested I take Spanish, perhaps because he needed a
few more students to fill his class. Apart from my father, I
don't believe I've ever met a kinder, more diplomatic
person. Although I had no aptitude for foreign languages,
I ended up taking four years of Spanish simply because I
liked being in the same room with this man. When I
returned to St. John's as a teacher, there was a story
circulating around campus illustrating how careful Father
Dunstan was to never offend anyone. It seems that the
administration, faced with the problem of how to reject

the application of the underachieving son of a prominent alumnus, turned to Father Dunstan to break the bad news to the family. So exceedingly diplomatic was the letter he wrote that the prominent alumnus answered by return mail, thanking Father Dunstan profusely for accepting his son, poor grades and all.

I particularly recall the funeral of Father Alfred, a colleague in the English department, because of the abbot's homily. I'd been in touch with Father Alfred for most of my adult life, for he, like I, was a fiction writer. At his funeral the abbot closed his eulogy by picturing him at work in the monastery vegetable garden. He said that when Alfred died he had finished harvesting the onions but hadn't gotten around to the carrots. This struck me as an eloquent commentary on the life of a monk. The life he leads is not totally spiritual or academic. And that has been a great part of the attraction for me, getting to know this community of men in all the phases of their lives—not only as teachers, but as fishermen, choristers, and gardeners. I found it inspiring, during the last seventeen years of my teaching career, to work with the monks—and with the sisters of St. Benedict's Monastery four miles away—because their dedication to their vocation is not unlike my own dedication to writing. Their lives have been examples for me.

Shortly after returning to live at St. John's in 1980, I was introduced to a member of the board of regents who said to me, "How come St. John's? I thought

Guggenheim fellows always took the money and went to Greece." This left me thinking about the writers I'd been reading who did go to Greece—Evelyn Waugh, Anthony Burgess, John Fowles—and I assumed it was more than the pleasing climate that drew them there. Tramping those rocky coastlines where literature and art and government and philosophy sprang up and flowered and seemed so fresh, they sought a kind of refreshment, getting in touch with the source of the culture we live in. And wasn't that what I was doing at St. John's, getting back to my beginnings? It was here, twenty-five years earlier, that my adult life sprang up and flowered and seemed so fresh, and now I was back like a pilgrim, for refreshment.

I discovered that St. John's is really three communities. There is the college, the monastery, and the seminary. My first year back I had a room in the seminary building. We were an autonomous community of four priests and forty seminarians on the upper floors, twenty college students renting rooms on the ground floor, and two or three oddballs like me who happened to have drifted onto campus in roles that weren't easy to call by name— the sort of mysterious hangers-on who have been a part of this community for a hundred years. I remember them from my student days, men with some tenuous and unspecified connection with St. John's who turned up out of nowhere and stayed for weeks or months. A few stayed for years. Some lie buried in the abbey cemetery.

The seminary was the ideal bolt-hole for me at this
time in my life. I had recently divorced my wife and felt
like hiding. For companionship I had the seminarians—
the kindest group of people I'd ever known. We took our
meals in a common dining room. I fell asleep to the
sound of murmuring and laughter down the hall. I
awoke to the sound of chanted prayer in the chapel.
Perhaps even more important than these creature comforts,
my casual conversations with the seminarians brought
me up-to-date with the church. I discovered that there
were really two churches. There was the church of the
small parishes I'd been a member of since leaving campus
in 1955, and there was the church of the theologian. The
parishes at that time were mostly administered by
autocratic priests who had been trained before Vatican II
and who delivered admonishing sermons with no sense
of their audience. At St. John's one was free to speculate
about the nature of God, of one's place in God's plan.
One did not come away from Mass with all the answers,
nor with a fear of eternal punishment.

I recall attending a student Mass in late November of
that year, when the readings were full of earthquakes and
darkness and howling wind and tears, prefiguring the
end of the world, and in turn prefiguring Advent and a
new beginning. The priest, a stranger to me, picked up
on the symbol of the earthquake and spoke to the students
about the stages in their lives when they lose, one by
one, the people and possessions and beliefs that seemed

so essential to them. His examples proved that he had a firm sense of his audience. He understood what the students were all going through—experiencing shifting thoughts concerning careers; realizing as seniors that majors that seemed appealing during the sophomore year were losing their appeal; coping with the death of parents, the pillars of our world; harboring unstable attitudes in an unstable world—and said we were in church that day searching for the rock of stability. And, best of all, he said it in ten minutes. I left deeply moved, and thankful that the modern priest is trained in homiletics.

St. John's is a rural campus, surrounded by deep woods and three lakes. I wasn't on campus very long before Father Hilary, prior of the monastery, took me out exploring the paths through the woods. A prior, being second in command, tends to the sort of administrative details that the abbot doesn't have time for. Whenever his paperwork got the best of him, Hilary called me up and suggested a walk. Having arrived on campus at eighteen, on the day the first atom bomb fell on Japan, he'd been walking these woods since 1945 and had found long trails I hadn't known existed, one of which I've never since been able to find on my own. "This is Tolkien country," he said one day, calling attention to the stillness and remoteness of this particular part of the forest—the soft carpet of decaying leaves, warm sunlight filtering down through the arching boughs, no sound but our voices. Hilary eventually became president of the college, a job that required him, in his words, "to spend alternate days among the rich," and thus left him no time for walks. And so I have gone back alone and stood at the point where I'm positive the Tolkien trail led off into the deep woods—and I've found no sign of it.

Surrounded by Birches

For the first twenty-five summers of my writing career, as soon as my teaching duties ended, I retreated to a small, clapboard cabin in the lake-dotted countryside of northern Minnesota, and there, from early June until Labor Day, I turned out most of my yearly quota of fiction. The place had belonged to my parents before it belonged to me, and they had built, on the same lot and surrounded by birch trees, a bunkhouse for guests, which I converted into my writing studio. Thus my companions were mostly figmentary people like Agatha McGee, Simon Shea, Fathers Frank Healy and James O'Hannon, who populated the novels that were on my mind day and night all summer. But I didn't completely lose touch with reality, for I had a few carefully chosen guests who came and stayed the three-night limit I set for them (on the fourth day my concentration began to unravel), as well as an indefatigable and unavoidable neighbor named Roy.

In the mid-1970s, Roy and his wife, Harriet, had retired from band-uniform sales in Nebraska and had moved into the insulated, year-round cabin next door to mine in order to relax on the lake. The trouble was that

Roy, the quintessential salesman, couldn't relax. Within
weeks of moving to the lake, he was on the road selling
tombstones to widows, wholesale liquor to bottle stores,
and baskets of fundraising fruit to high schools. For the
annual civic celebration called Muskie Days in the nearby
village of Nevis, he canvassed all the merchants in the
larger town of Park Rapids, gathering prizes to raffle off
during the outdoor stage show, and because he got so
many more prizes than could possibly be given away in
one evening, he held back the extras for his own use as
well as for bartering items for goods and services. I can
still hear his voice calling to me as he came hurrying
across the yard between our cabins: "Jon, here's a certifi-
cate for a nice steak dinner at the Antlers Cafe with your
name on it—can I borrow your lawn mower?" or "Jon,
here's an oil change at the Shell station—my son and his
family are coming up from Omaha for the weekend and
we'd like to use your boat."

He was a small man, sloppy and crude and entirely
lovable. He was one of those people whose clothes
never fit. He could put on a tailored sport coat for
church on Sunday morning, and within minutes one
sleeve would appear inches longer than the other, and
his shirt would be askew—and freshly stained with
tobacco, because although he'd quit smoking cigars
years earlier, he continued to chew them and drooled.
As a classic and horrible example of his crudeness, at
lunch one day as Harriet passed me the pickle dish and

asked if I'd care for some, he said, "Sure he will—Jon'll eat anything that'll make a turd."

Roy's lovableness grew out of his childlike candor and vulnerability. He interrupted my writing one day to tell me, "You know, I've got a lot of insecurities. I'm afraid of dogs and I'm afraid of night."

"You're seventy years old and afraid of night?" I was incredulous.

"Oh, yes, I can't stand to be alone when it gets dark—I'm afraid I'll die at night. One night Harriet left me alone and went to the neighbor's to play cards, and I got so scared I called her up and told her I was afraid of dying."

"What did she say?"

"Oh, you know Harriet." By which he meant she was the stoical one in the family. "She said, 'Well, if you die you won't know it' and hung up."

She was stoical all right. Coming home one sunny August afternoon from the hospital where Roy had had heart surgery, she stopped by my cabin and announced his death by calling through my screen door, "Your neighbor didn't make it."

Whether or not he knew he died, I was glad he did it in daylight.

🌱

Among my annual summer visitors was my friend Bob, who was the academic dean at St. John's. It was Bob who had invited me to spend my Guggenheim year (1980–81) at St. John's, a place I couldn't bear to leave until I retired in 1997. As dean, he was by far the best administrator I ever worked for. He was a swift and voracious reader, conversant with almost all disciplines. Every day he came to campus with a briefcase full of articles for his faculty's edification and dispatched them to our mailboxes all over campus. He was also the wittiest man I ever knew. He's been dead six years now, and still I hear from people who say they miss Bob.

Besides myself, Bob was the only other person I've known who seemed obsessed with trying to get his every thought down on paper. Upon arriving for his first visit at the lake (before the age of word processors) he set up his typewriter in the main cabin and spent three days churning out articles and book reviews while I proceeded with my fiction in the bunkhouse. I was unaware of the effect of the noise of two writers at work until Bob drove away and Roy immediately came over to tell me, "Jon, do you realize that Harriet and I moved up here from Nebraska to hear the birds singing in the trees, and yet all we hear seven days a week is the clickety clack of your goddam typewriter. So we're always glad to see you get company because then you let up on the typing at least for a little while, but this weirdo, he types all day along with you, and we can't hear a goddam thing except the two of you going clickety clack, clickety clack."

Clever remarks must be the most ephemeral things we utter, because I cannot now think of even one example, but I remember so well the time I spent touring Italy and England with Bob and his wife, Betty, and being constantly buoyed by his witty observations virtually every time we turned a corner. As one of his friends said at his funeral, "He was simply the most upbeat man we knew."

Then I watched him sink. In 1993, he and his wife separated. In 1994, he traveled to Greece with a student group, but had to leave them in the hands of his fellow guide and flew home in a state of fatigue. He had a heart condition. He was hospitalized for a month, given a pacemaker, and finally sent home as a potential candidate for a heart transplant. On his third day home, two friends dropped in and found him sitting on the floor watching the news. They were struck by his weakened condition, his apathetic attitude, and they stepped into his kitchen to discuss whether to summon an ambulance. Bob called to them, "Come back in here. I need conversation." Those were his last words, for they found him lying dead on the floor.

How typical of him to say he needed not medical attention, but conversation, for Bob was all brain, as well as the most gregarious man I've ever known. He had a blind spot where physicality was concerned. He seemed impervious to every emotion except loneliness. I had been present in his house as a late-night party was breaking up and Bob stood pleading with his guests not to go home. "I hate it when everybody leaves," he said. It was this need for human contact that had made him such good company, such a good dean, such a good man.

&

Joe, another of my guests at the cabin, has never had a silent thought. He wakes up talking, and as long as someone's within earshot, keeps it up all day, all of it delivered at high volume and punctuated with raucous laughter. A three-day visit wasn't long enough to tell me everything he needed to say, so he'd pull into the yard in his butterscotch Toyota with a written agenda, important topics listed first—say the twelve plays he'd seen on his last ten-day visit to London, or the movies he'd been to since his last visit to my cabin—and trailing off through lesser matters, such as gossip from Brainerd Community College, where he and I were colleagues for twelve years and where he continues to teach.

For Joe is a famously good teacher. He's a bald, gray-bearded bachelor who for the past thirty-five years has lived out his life in the classroom. He loves his students so dearly that he hugs each of them as they leave his English class. He's an indiscriminate hugger. One day I watched an elderly man, a visitor to campus, step out of the college library, across the hall from Joe's classroom, and walk, befuddled, into Joe's embrace.

Thirty years ago, before it caught on around the nation, Joe was teaching human relations in his Composition class, and he was doing it in unorthodox ways. If you saw blindfolded students groping along the hallway, for example, you knew they were studying something—surely not English—with Joe. Most of the rest of us in the department were outraged that Joe's students should be having fun while ours were making hard work of learning their grammar. Were we envious that his classes were so hugely popular, or why did we call a meeting at which Joe was accused of sidestepping the chore of teaching writing while providing his students with nothing but entertainment? We'd even seen candles burning in his classroom. And what about the auction he'd conducted from the stage of the theater last month, the Maypole dance last spring? We were a department of five instructors, four against one.

Joe stood his ground. He was teaching communication, he insisted, and he was doing so in creative ways. And, by the way, he was doing it over and above his job of teaching writing—which he proved by showing us a pile of compositions, each with his editing marks apparent on the page. This of course rendered our objections rather hollow, so we tried a different approach. Because his course was such a departure from the traditional way of teaching, it oughtn't be called Composition. Its title should be a signal to students of what they were in for.

Far from objecting to this idea, Joe eagerly—and laughingly—embraced it. As a person who'd always marched to a different drummer, he was glad not to be harnessed to that stodgy old freight wagon of Composition. And so that's why, to this day, the classes that fill up first on registration day are called "Creative Communication."

🌱

Eight miles west of my cabin lies the town of Park Rapids, where I spent six years (1959–65) teaching English to the high-school seniors. Of the six schools and colleges I taught at, this is the only one where, for years afterward, I kept in touch with many of my former students. I did this by living at the edge of that community. I would drive into town nearly every afternoon for a cup of coffee and a change of scene when my writing stint was finished, and the local newspaper or a conversation or a face across the street brought me up-to-date on a person from out of my past. Whereas in the other towns my students ceased to exist the moment I gave them their final grades, these people lived lives beyond English class. One called me up every six months or so for several years, teetering on the brink of alcoholism and despair. Another phoned from Wisconsin, where she had just divorced the husband she had put through medical school. Still another stopped me on the street to tell me about his cancer operation. Even now, two women from that time in my life turn up at my house in Minneapolis each week to help me straighten out my office, my files, this manuscript.

8

j. f. powers and betty wahl

Making a Shirt

Studying the sketches in this book, I find that while
most of the good people have done good deeds for
others, there is a type of person whose goodness grows
out of a dedication to a worthy principle. My boyhood
friend Jackie is an example, for it was simply his selfless
nature I found so inspiring. My character Simon Shea
is another; in his dedication to his marriage vow, he
forces the reader to ponder the sacredness of making a
promise. Still another is Connor in *Rookery Blues,* a painter
dedicated entirely to his art. Here follows a study of two
people who, in concentrating single-mindedly on their
writing, became rather abrasive toward the neighbors, but
who left behind six very good books for generations of
readers to enjoy.

J. F. Powers was a man of few and carefully chosen
words. I remember my first conversation with him. It
was one-sided and lasted about six seconds. I had recently
come to teach at St. John's University, and as I crossed
the campus one morning, he fell into step beside me.
This was twenty-one winters ago.

"I read your new book," he said.

I was flattered speechless to think that Powers,
whose peerless first novel, *Morte d'Urban,* had won the
National Book Award in 1963, not only recognized the
new novelist on campus, but had actually read *The Love
Hunter.* I couldn't wait to hear his opinion, which he
quickly imparted:

"I liked parts of it," he said, and turned a corner and was gone.

He was an eminently quotable speaker. One day I was invited to hear him speak to a colleague's class of English majors, where he read to them from an Ann Landers column—a marriage problem—and declared it the raw material of fiction. "This is your cotton growing in the fields," he said, waving the clipping in the air. "Take it and make a shirt."

Later he was asked if his priest novels were mostly for Catholic readers. He replied, "Is *Wind in the Willows* mostly for animals?"

Powers died in June 1999 at his home near campus. Although we were colleagues for almost twenty years, I never felt close to him, for he was a single-minded loner, devoting his life entirely to his writing and holding himself aloof from his colleagues. He had been, at midcentury, perhaps the most famous Catholic writer in America. He and his wife, the writer Betty Wahl (who preceded him in death by eleven years), were the best examples I've ever met of people whose dedication to a principle resulted in a legacy of great value. Their principle was writing fiction, and their legacy to the readers of the world (an endangered species in their opinion) is, in his case, three story collections, *Prince of Darkness, The Presence of Grace,* and *Look How the Fish Live,* and two novels, *Morte d'Urban* and *Wheat That Springeth Green*; and in hers, a number of short stories published in such periodicals as

The New Yorker and *The Kenyon Review* and a novel entitled *Rafferty and Co.*

Pal or Chum

Powers was a famously secretive writer—a fact that I, in my eagerness to know what he was working on, never learned to respect. Time after time (despite his favorite response, "Let's not talk about it") I would ask him about his work in progress. It was in the campus post office one afternoon that he finally leveled with me. "This is my editor at Knopf," he said, holding up a piece of mail. "He's wondering where my novel is."

"Aha," said I, "so it's a novel, is it?" (He had already published his three story collections and one novel.)

"A novel overdue at my publishers," he admitted.

"How long overdue?"

"Thirteen years," he said.

It isn't hard for me to believe that Powers had spent every day of those many overdue years working on the novel, for he was simply the most deliberate writer I've ever known or heard of. One Christmas season I went to his office with one of his books and asked him to autograph it as a gift. "What shall I say?" he asked.

" 'Best wishes to Harriet,' would be fine." I suggested. Whereupon he took an old letter from his desk drawer, wrote a first draft of this greeting on the back of the envelope, looked it over, nodded his approval, and copied it into the book.

Another time, visiting my class, he was asked by a student, "What did you write this morning?"

"Writing isn't only writing, it's also thinking," he explained, maybe sardonically, maybe not. "I spent this morning trying to determine whether a certain character would say 'pal' or 'chum.'"

"Which did you choose?" asked the student.

"I haven't decided yet."

He was in fine form that day. He depressed us all with his eloquent description of the decline of civilization in general and in literacy in particular. The shrinking audience for serious fiction. The sad shape of the economy at that time. The threat of nuclear war. He kept bringing up authors who were important to him—Waugh, Mauriac, Joyce—and saying to the class, "Of course none of you have ever heard of this."

He spoke about his story "Keystone" (which my class had read), written on the momentum left over after *Morte d'Urban*. He said he'd had only two or three periods like that in his life, when he was so deep in his fiction that he was capable of very good things. The first time, when he was writing "Lions, Harts, Leaping Does" (my favorite story), he worked so long and hard that he damaged his eyesight. Next class, I asked for reactions. One young woman said she'd lived next door to Powers most of her life and this was the most she had ever heard him say.

Another young woman resented his disdain for the

class, his repeating, "Of course you've never heard of this book, this author." She was immediately challenged by several of her classmates, who said, "But he's right, we haven't read those books, we haven't heard of half of those authors."

All That Money

The first time I was invited to Powers's house it was to meet the novelist Frederick Manfred. They got down to fundamental questions right away, such as how were they sleeping these days, and where had all the readers gone? Manfred was a blustery, earnest, and prodigious talker; Powers a wry, self-deprecating comedian:

Powers: "How's your wife?"

Manfred: "My wife and I were divorced about five years ago."

"Oh, I didn't know that."

"She's a brilliant woman, but after thirty years the areas we agreed on got to be fewer and fewer and we decided to part. She's doing all right. She got quite an inheritance."

"Can't you get her back?"

"Well, as a matter of fact, she talks about coming back, but I know it wouldn't work."

"But she's got that money. I think you should try to get her back."

"No, no, I'm looking around. I've got a new house

two-thirds built. It's at the point now where I can have a
lady in and she wouldn't find it uncomfortable."

"A lady with money?"

"No, not necessarily."

"I think you should try to get your wife back. All that
money."

Later, they got around to the topic of writing. Manfred,
at seventy-one, had just finished novel number twenty-
five and knew what the next four were going to be about.
Then he intended to start on his nonfiction.

Manfred: "Do you write in the evening?"

Powers: "No, hardly ever."

"You go to bed early?"

"No, I go to bed at one-thirty and get up at nine. I
get to my office around eleven. I fiddle around. I come
home around five."

"What time do you do your best writing?"

"Never."

Bach and Woody Herman

Compared to Powers, his wife was the next most
deliberate writer I've ever known. Betty Wahl (her
maiden and pen name) had published *Rafferty and Co.,*
a novel based on one of their extended sojourns in
Ireland, as well as several short stories. Her first *New
Yorker* story, in fact, had predated Jim's by a year or two
in the late forties.

J. F. Powers and Betty Wahl

Betty, too, had an exacting mind. She whispered to me in the campus library one day that she'd read my latest novel, *A Green Journey.* "I'm not sure you're correct about there being Holstein cattle in Ireland," she said. "I'll write and ask my son, in Dublin. He's in college there, hoping to find ultimate truth by studying Spinoza."

It was perhaps a month later that we met again, and she reported that there were indeed Holsteins in Ireland.

"And how about your son?" I asked. "Has he found what he was looking for?"

"No, he's still searching. I wrote and told him there is no ultimate truth." Then she added with pride, "He wrote back to say that I contradicted myself."

Uncompromising in her speech, she preferred, like her husband, the clean, swift cut. When my father died, in 1984, Betty said to me, "Well, Jon, you're one step closer to the brink."

When Sister Mariella Gable died at nearby St. Benedict's Monastery, I went to her wake primarily (I have to admit) to witness the reaction of Jim and Betty, for it had been Sister Mariella who had brought them together. This nun, a nationally recognized scholar of Catholic writers who had struck up a correspondence with Powers in the 1940s, had soon after sent him several pages of fiction by her most promising student. Impressed with the writing, he replied that he would like to meet the writer, whereupon she invited him to address her class, introduced him to Betty, and not long after that they were married.

After prayers in the chapel, and accompanied by an organ fugue by Bach, we processed into the adjoining gathering room to view Sister Mariella's body. I got in line behind the Powerses in order to hear what they might say. Jim, having glanced at the corpse, turned to Betty and said, "I hate Bach more than anybody except Woody Herman."

A Vocation of Poverty

"I never show Betty my work anymore," Powers told me at a college social function in the spring of 1988. "Whenever we share our work with each other, we fight." He went on to say that he was having a student type the final draft of his second novel, *Wheat That Springeth Green,* and he was worried about telling Betty, who had been planning to type it. Meanwhile across the room, Betty was telling my wife that Jim was having a student type his manuscript in order to save her the stress of doing so.

One day I found myself caught in the crossfire of their anger. I had invited Betty to be one of a series of authors visiting campus, but when her turn came, she'd undergone an operation for intestinal cancer and was too sick to appear. Instead of canceling her reading I asked if I might present a couple of her stories to the audience. After all, it had been many years since her last story was published and most people I knew were not aware of her work. She agreed and invited me to their house to pick up the stories.

Entering the house that winter day, I sensed what a colleague had meant when he described the Powerses as "making a vocation of poverty." The place was poorly insulated and chilly. Apparently to save her the exertion of climbing to the second floor, Betty's bed (which was to be her deathbed a few months later) was a cot in the dining room. She spoke candidly of her illness, and when I asked if she was in pain, she said, "Yes, but it doesn't matter, because I know the cause. It's unidentified pain that drives you crazy."

Her husband came in for lunch as she was handing me three stories to choose from—one from *The New Yorker,* one from *McCall's,* and the third from *The Kenyon Review.* He told her not to let me read the *McCall's* story, and when she disagreed, he grew angry, insisting, "But it's not a good story, Betty. It's badly written." The argument went on for a couple of embarrassing minutes before he concluded it with "Oh, go ahead, it's your life!" and stalked out of the room.

They were united, however, in their determination not to accept payment for their readings; whether out of some sort of loyalty to St. John's or a chronic disdain for money, I don't know. When I mentioned that she would get the normal fee of $250, she seemed horrified. "Don't you dare pay me," she said, and reprimanded me for having earlier given Jim, for his reading, a stereo album of pieces by Duke Ellington, his favorite composer and musician.

"Not even a bouquet of flowers?" I asked.

"No," she insisted, shuddering at the thought. "Cut flowers are my idea of hell."

A Saint with a Bad Temper

One day in 1987 Powers complained to me about television. It seems that Betty's mother, who was very old, had moved in with them, and because she missed her programs, he had bought his first TV. He said she turned it on in the morning and left it on all day. "The sound of it is horrible. And the shows! Why, there's one called 'Wheel of Fortune,' in which adults are actually playing a children's game."

"How about 'The Price Is Right?'" I said. "Don't you think that's worse?"

"I'm no expert," he said, as if I were.

Television was part of a larger problem for Powers: American culture was being corrupted on every side— popular music, popular reading habits, public morality. In 1975, having come home from his longest stay in Ireland with his family, he said, on a radio interview I happened to hear, that he was puzzled by the appearance of America's denim-clad youngsters. "Why are all these people wearing blue clothes?" he asked. "And why are they all walking around with cans of soda pop in their hands?" Later, when I asked what prompted him to remain so long in Ireland, he said, again with a hint of facetiousness in his eye, "Some dumb-sounding young fellow with adenoids telephoned the house and asked to speak with my eldest daughter, so we left the country for twelve years."

This daughter, Katherine Anne (named after her godmother, Katherine Anne Porter), I met at Betty's funeral in May 1988. Betty's brother, Father Thomas Wahl, a Benedictine monk of St. John's Abbey, said the Mass. In his homily he quoted extensively from letters Betty had written to him over the years. Afterward, among the many mourners invited to Jim's house, I said to Katherine, "That was a very good eulogy your uncle delivered."

"It should have been," she said, in the clipped manner of her parents. "My mother wrote most of it."

Before the funeral, in the vestibule of the church, I had overheard Jim say to a friend, "Betty wrote the menu every day and I went into the kitchen and tried to cook all that crap." Afterward, in his house, he took me aside to describe the scene at breakfast the day of her death.

"She'd been having either chicken liver or eggs for breakfast for some time, but that morning when I asked if she wanted an egg or liver, she said, 'I won't answer that question.' So I went out and made a paper ballot, 'egg' with a box to check, 'liver' with a box to check, and I gave her that with a pencil. She looked it over and said she wouldn't vote. So I went out and added a third choice. I added 'kisses' with a box to check and I gave her that. She studied it and smiled and then she drew a diagonal line—half an X—through the box next to liver. 'You have to draw the other half,' I said. She shook her head. 'Yes, you do,' I told her. 'Otherwise they won't understand it in the kitchen.' She drew the line, and I cooked the liver. She ate it and threw it up about half an hour later."

He added, after a thoughtful pause, "Betty was a saint. A saint with a bad temper." And then, as if fearing that he'd revealed a bit of tenderness, he looked about him at the crowd of people in his house and said, "It was good she died when she did. I'm in need of a family gathering in my novel. I'll be sitting down to write about this scene at four o'clock this afternoon."

A Man Adrift

Betty's death was followed by that of Jim's closest friend, the artist Joe O'Connell. After that Jim seemed like a man adrift. On his daily walk to the campus post office he kept his eyes on the ground, an expression of defiance drawn tightly on his face. Once you broke through to him you found the same warm and spirited conversationalist as before, but few people made the attempt, so forbidding was his stern façade. Some thought this facade meant he was concentrating, composing fiction in his head, but I believe it was—in addition to his chronic shyness—a case of loneliness and depression.

One particularly frigid and dismal January day, I dropped in for a visit and found his house, without

Betty, even more austere than before. He had hung rugs and blankets on the walls to keep the wind from blowing through his living room. A very small Christmas tree stood decorated on a table, and under it a few gifts with their wrapping still intact. Pointing to them I said, "Your presents, Jim."

"Yes, I know. It's such a lot of bother opening presents."

"But people will be expecting thank-you notes."

"Oh, I've already written them," he said wearily.

As far as I know, Powers presented only two public readings from his second novel and final book, *Wheat That Springeth Green* (1988), one in St. Paul and the other, which I attended, at St. John's. He read the first two chapters, based on his own boyhood in Jacksonville, Illinois. The first, entitled "See Me," is restricted to a three year old's consciousness and is reminiscent of the opening of Joyce's *Portrait of the Artist as a Young Man*. Past his bedtime, the toddler, Joe, keeps coming downstairs, attracted by a party his parents are hosting. Trying out various lines on the guests, he finds that "I eat cheese" charms them as much as any, and so he repeats it again and again.

Powers looked up only long enough to tell us, "I myself did that at three," and then he plunged into chapter two, reading in his customary smooth and quiet monotone about the ten-year-old Joe, who had become the favorite Mass server of a gruff pastor and a hard-drinking curate. Listening, I was struck by what little space he devoted to physical description; his strength was in writing what people thought and said.

He said the book was motivated in part by the public's ignorance regarding priests. What kind of man becomes a priest? What kind of man is a priest? Asked to account for his lifelong interest in the priesthood, he said he was fascinated by these men who had the impossible job of balancing the practical life with the spiritual; one foot in this life, the other foot in the world to come.

Entertaining God

Jim died in 1999, at the age of 81—notwithstanding his determination to grow as old as his father, who had choked on a piece of meat and died at 103. Given his elusiveness, we shouldn't have been surprised when, upon entering the St. John's Abbey Church for Jim's funeral, we found him absent. He had been buried three days earlier at a graveside service. Betty's brother, Fr. Thomas, again said the Mass. He described, among other things, Jim's reactionary opinions concerning the present-day church. Pointing to the place at the center of Marcel Breuer's vast (and acoustically troublesome) balcony, he said, "That's where Jim sat, Sunday after Sunday, and when he was asked why, he said it was the only place in the entire church where he couldn't hear anything."

He spoke of Jim's frustrations as a novelist, and I recalled Jim's remarks about the chore of writing. On revising: "I know a page is satisfactory when it doesn't make me throw up anymore." On recovering from poor reviews: "When you get knocked out of the ring, it takes courage to climb back in." Moreover, he had been suffering through the ultimate frustration that every writer fears most: he died with all of his books—two novels and three story collections—out of print.

His will specified that there be no music at this Mass, except the lovely hymn "Wheat That Springeth Green," which we sang after the homily:

> Now the green blade riseth, from the buried grain,
> Wheat that in the dark earth many days has lain;
> Love lives again, that with the dead has been:
> Love has come again, like wheat that springeth green.

We weren't a great crowd of mourners, something fewer than 150 in number, which included a couple of celebrities—Garrison Keillor and Eugene McCarthy. Filing out of church, we stood around in the June sunshine shaking hands, which, out of respect for Jim's disdain for the practice, we'd been asked to refrain from doing before Communion. It occurred to me then that St. John's, the center of liturgical renewal in the United States, had lost its last enemy of change. And of course we had lost much more. We had lost our best writer and our most quotable eccentric. And, according to a recent article I'd read, we had lost a theologian as well: "There is a common quality in all art—it has something to do with God-given spirit, going beyond oneself," Powers had told a pair of students who interviewed him for the campus literary magazine. Knowing of his taste in music, they had asked him if a parallel could be drawn between jazz and writing.

> Really good paintings, sculpture, music, writing—they all have it. I can't name it, but I think it's possible to write something, for me to write something, that even God might like. It's possible for me to hit a note, to get in a mood, to write something that is worthy of God's attention. Not as a soul seeking salvation, but just as entertainment for God. This may be blasphemous to say, but I believe it. I don't think God is there and we're here —there are connections. I think there are connections and I think art is certainly one. I think that's true of really good jazz. When you'd hear the Ellington band . . . oh! . . . you'd get shivers! It's—so damn good! There's a connection.

Leaving campus after the funeral, I drove past the cemetery, where, without waiting for our blessing, Jim had at last joined Betty, whose grave he had visited almost daily for the past eleven years.

Hardball Elegance

Scarcely a year after his death, all of Jim's published work —*Morte d'Urban, Wheat That Springeth Green,* and *The Stories*—was back in print, thanks to the editors of the Classics series at New York Review Books, and I am captivated all over again by his writing style. As Donna Tartt says in her review in *Harper's* (July 2000),

> Every sentence is a marvel, clear and polished, always surprising, with a comedic bite. . . . The resulting prose is pure American, as tough and nervy in its way as the prose of Raymond Chandler but tempered throughout with a gorgeous precision and acidity. . . . Its particular flavor of hardball elegance seems to me quite original.

I am struck by Jim's alertness as a writer. He never put his prose on automatic pilot. As a shrewd observer, he knew where he was going, subtly choosing the precise, and sometimes surprising, word at all times. In his story "The Old Bird," for example, the word "superior." His elderly protagonist, a man named Newman, enters an employment office, looks about him at the others, who, like he is, are unemployed, and notices: "They all had that superior look of people out of work." As a further example of Powers's smooth handling of a subtle situation, the old man's interviewer, a Mr. Shanahan, offers him a job in the mail room, a step down from the office work he's been used to.

> For an instant Mr. Newman succeeded [by his facial expression] in making it plain that he, like any man of his business experience, was meant for better things. A moment later, in an interesting ceremony which took place in his heart, Mr. Newman surrendered his well-loved white collar. He knew that Mr. Shanahan, with that dark vision peculiar to personnel men, had witnessed the whole thing.

Although his favorite topic is the Catholic priesthood, none of Powers's work comes across as particularly religious. It's not pietistic or sentimental. The rite of holy orders doesn't diminish his priests' humanity, their faults, their weaknesses. While Father Urban (the main character of *Morte d'Urban* and Powers's most fully realized creation) works unstintingly to promote his small, impoverished order, the Clementines, he reveals himself to be a proud and ambitious social climber—until the end of the novel, when, hospitalized by an accident on the golf course, he renounces his self-centered ways. Some of the Clementines feel betrayed, of course, by this change in their hotshot fund-raiser, but Urban at last becomes the ideal monk, humble and self-effacing rather than self-serving.

In story after story and in both of his novels, his clergy are compromised by unethical colleagues or parishioners, by officious bishops, by overbearing house-keepers, or by their own addiction to the bottle. But in every story there is an ideal of goodness that, though often unattainable, is at least a goal to shoot for, or a standard by which to measure failure.

Jim's view of life I'd characterize as antimaterialist conservative. Change is upsetting in a number of stories. So are the ugliness of our shopping malls, the impersonality of our employers, our preoccupation with getting money and spending it. Betty, however, seems ambivalent on this subject. In a story called "Gingerbread," she describes the case of a teaching nun, representing the old order of things, whose stitchery classes are sadly elbowed out of the classroom by the influx of students who are enamored of a bright young sister. In *Rafferty and Co.,* on the other hand, she portrays the old order as anachronistic and harmful. In this novel, expanded from a short story by the same name published in *The Kenyon Review,* she portrays the Raffertys moving from America to Ireland in order to expand the family textile business by setting up an Irish branch for the production of wool. As Mrs. Rafferty tends to the household and the children, Mr. Rafferty makes it his business to become acquainted with the natives, mostly in pubs, where he spends more and more of his time until, at the end, he becomes an idle barfly like his new friends and the textile idea comes to nothing.

As far back as 1956, the critic Alfred Kazin described Powers as "subtle, funny, precise, and always unexpected. . . . He is a miniaturist, a close thinker, close as a chess player at times." At times almost too close, it seems to me. He sometimes overdoes the subtlety. His characters are oddly reticent, and so is the author. In "Tinkers," for example, his only story set in Ireland, he portrays an American called Daddy who, moving to a small town outside Dublin with Mama and their five children, becomes fascinated by the nomadic, mendicant, gypsy-like people called tinkers. One morning, listening to the radio, he learns that the tinkers

> have often caused friction, particularly in Limerick and Dublin suburbs, where residents claim that they indulge in fighting and leave a large amount of litter. . . ." Nothing new here, nothing for him. "There are six main tinker tribes." Oh? "The

Stokeses, Joyces, McDonaghs, Wards"—Now wait a minute—"and Redmonds."

So the odds against him were greater than he thought. He took the next train into Dublin, left the *Irish Times* on it, and gave the first tinker woman he met a coin, wanting and not wanting to know her name.

From this we are to gather that the fifth name in the list is Daddy's own. Perhaps an astute reader might figure this out from the rest of the story (in which Daddy's family, moving from house to house, comes to resemble the tinkers), but I missed it until I heard Powers explain it one time in a radio interview.

This reticence, or hypersubtlety, turns up often enough to spoil, for me, whole chapters of *Wheat That Springeth Green*. The protagonist of this novel, a pastor named Joe, is given a new curate whose name—through a bureaucratic mix-up in the chancery office—he doesn't know. Fully twenty pages are devoted to Joe's surreptitious attempts to learn the young man's name. In my opinion, Joe's refusal to ask him directly drains the comedy from this section. When he finally learns the name—it's Bill—Joe explains himself to Bill this way:

> I was trying to save us both embarrassment. I didn't want you to think what you would've—of me, of the Church, of yourself. I didn't want you to think you didn't matter, Bill. And I don't want you to think that now. So don't. This is all [Chancellor] Toohey's fault. God help the diocese if they don't make a bishop of him pretty soon. He's doing untold harm where he is now.

This supposedly clears the air, and, the air cleared, we are finally able to move on to a more interesting phase of the relationship between a jaded pastor and an inept curate.

But I'm quibbling about a very small matter, considering the magnitude and beauty of Powers's work overall.

> In story after story [as Kazin says] the space in which we move is one of "gravity," but the victory that is won is one of grace. Gravity . . . is the fatal ordinariness of life that brings everybody down, even priests. The point that he makes so quietly is that clerical housekeeping gets as muddled as any other. . . . And grace? The point about grace is that it is always mysterious. Its presence is a gift.
> What an original Mr. Powers is, and what a true writer he seems on the American scene.

9

the good, the bad, and the saintly

Fictional Friends and Enemies

Somewhere in Yeats—I forget which poem—is the phrase "perfection of the life or of the work." It's a reference to the artist's having to choose, in Yeats's opinion, which will take precedence—living a normal life or devoting one's primary energies to one's art. For the first fifteen or twenty years of my writing career, I chose the latter. I sometimes felt like Proust at the moment he decided to retire and spend the rest of his time on earth describing it, turning his back on all his friends and going to work:

> So far from going into society, I would not even per-
> mit people to come and see me at home . . . for the
> duty of writing my book took precedence now over
> that of being polite or even kind. . . . I should have
> the courage to reply to those who came to see me or
> tried to get me to visit them that I had, for necessary
> business which required my immediate attention, a
> supremely important appointment with myself. . . .
>
> How much more worth living did life appear to
> me now, now that I seemed to see that this life that
> we live in half-darkness can be illumined, this life
> that we distort can be restored to its true and pristine
> shape, that a life, in short, can be realized within the
> confines of a book.

I have experienced, along with periods of loneliness, the pleasure of having nothing but fiction in my mind for days at a time to the exclusion of human contact. Most of the time, the people I invented seemed adequate company, par-ticularly those who displayed a particular sort of goodness, such as Father Adrian Lawrence in *North of Hope.*

Father Lawrence is goodness personified. He's an otherworldly sort of priest who's been preaching the same theme from the pulpit for years—loving-kindness. He spends a good bit of his day praying for a staggering list of souls in purgatory. I tried to keep him from being cloyingly good by picturing him through the eyes of the younger priests of the diocese, who think him a silly old fogey and have nicknamed him "Loving Kindness." Here he is, early one chilly spring morning, sitting in a lawn chair with a copy of *Life* magazine and praying for the souls of the departed.

> "God bless Elvis Presley . . . and God bless Sir Anthony Eden." . . . His copy of *Life* was a year-end issue he'd found at the barber's yesterday and asked permission to borrow, because it contained photos of the many celebrities who had died during the past year and he couldn't be sure they'd left behind soulmates to pray for them. He leafed through it now, searching for the obituary section. "James M. Cain," he said when he located it. He sipped his lukewarm coffee and added, "Joan Crawford and Werner von Braun, may you rest in peace."
>
> Adrian was turning to the next page of dead people when he saw Frank coming across the yard from his schoolchildren's Mass. Frank was pastor now.
>
> "Good morning, Adrian."
>
> "Ah, Frank my boy, look here. Did you know that Bing Crosby, Ethel Waters, and Guy Lombardo all got away from us in the same year?"
>
> Frank took the magazine and scanned the pictures. "And Groucho Marx."
>
> Adrian chuckled.

"And Gary Gilmore," Frank added.

Adrian frowned. "Yes, executed. Let's hope our Lord is healing him with his loving kindness."

But who's to say that Adrian Lawrence, in his innocence, is a better person than those who have to overcome obstacles to goodness? I think of Miles Pruitt, Simon Shea, and Agatha McGee. Miles Pruitt in *Staggerford* is the quintessential teacher who, despite his ennui, pours his efforts into his students while maintaining just enough of a cynical nature to put up with Staggerford High School's oafish administration. His talent as a teacher lies primarily in his ability to listen. Leaving his classroom one day, one of his students, Beverly Bingham, pauses to tell him of her personal problems and suddenly breaks into tears.

> "Goddam it," she said, "I told myself I wasn't going to cry today." She stepped back into the classroom and put her books on Miles's desk and sobbed silently into the short sleeve of her soiled blouse.
>
> Miles couldn't think of anything to say. His words of solace were blurted out in choppy phrases that he himself did not entirely understand, but which— the wonder of it—Beverly seemed to find valuable. She wiped her face and smiled at him through her tears. She picked up her books and went to the door, then turned and said, "I'm sorry, but you're the one I had to tell because you always seem to have your shit together."

In eventually steering Miles into a situation where he gives his life in an effort to save one of his students from harm, I intended—consciously or not—to portray him as a sacrificial lamb in a profession that will consume everything you have, if you let it. I was probably feeling quite depleted myself when I wrote *Staggerford,* having just completed my twentieth year in the classroom.

My second novel, *Simon's Night,* is about vows. Simon Peter Shea, a devout Catholic, stubbornly assumes that his marriage vow is a lifelong commitment even though his wife left him years ago. Whatever I thought about his fidelity—and sometimes it struck me as foolish—I loved Simon for being a strict follower of his conscience. Remembering a love affair he had terminated some years ago because he felt himself a married man, he tries to explain himself to a young friend named Douglas:

> Of all my faculties— my memory, my will, my appetites, my reason—it's my conscience that dominates."
>
> "That must be hell."
>
> "It has its compensations. You have a sense of living your life within a prescribed set of rules. Your life has direction, a destiny in eternity. And of course you're never troubled by doubt or indecision where morality is concerned."
>
> "Sounds like you're a victim of your conscience. Not your own man."
>
> "I would say servant, Douglas, rather than victim. And a servant enjoys a peace of mind that a master does not. . . . The master must continually decide. The servant merely acts on those decisions." . . .
>
> "But that's childish."
>
> "Not childish. Childlike, perhaps, but not childish."

Agatha McGee, my most popular character among my readers, is a complicated mix of goodness and officiousness. She likes to maintain her own privacy while delving into the lives of her neighbors and friends and making sure they are walking the narrow and decorous path to salvation. She never doubts herself. She's always right. This overbearing type of neighborliness may be part of what makes her appealing, for in a world of ambiguities we admire definiteness. But then, just when you're convinced of her autocratic high-handedness, she will perform an act of pure kindness, allowing her innate goodness to show through. Taking in needy people to live with her—Beverly Bingham in *Staggerford,* Janet Raft in *A Green Journey,* her nephew Frederick Lopat in *Dear James*—is an example. Forgiving Imogene Kite's betrayal at the end of *Dear James* is another.

Witnessing Agatha's struggles with her conscience over moral issues is another part of her appeal, at least for me. I have enjoyed watching her confront certain ambiguous situations. In both *A Green Journey* and *Dear James* she finds herself, at sixty-eight, in love with a priest, of all things. In my current novel-in-progress, she feels obliged to tell a very big lie in an attempt to save the neighboring village of Willoughby from disintegrating. Fearing that she's put her eternal salvation in jeopardy in order to save the livelihoods of several citizens of Willoughby, she tries to justify herself by looking to history, and to Abraham Lincoln, for precedent. "Did saving the Union from disintegration offset the terrible sin of starting the Civil War, in which millions of men died? Evidently it did, for she couldn't imagine Lincoln in hell."

Both Frank Healy in *North of Hope* and Leland Edwards in *The Dean's List* are people I admire for their fortitude in struggling through the thickets of their professions—Frank in the priesthood, Leland in education—without losing their integrity. Frank Healy serves his flock while overcoming a kind of depression he calls his "big leak." He first felt it in the pulpit, where he stood

> dumb as a post. Terribly embarrassing. More than embarrassing—frightening.
>
> His first sign of the big leak. . . . A gradual decline in his articulateness, a deadening of his wit. The church was filled with unease as he opened his mouth to speak and nothing came out. He didn't prolong the anxiety, his or his congregation's. He silently blessed them, went back to the altar, and took up the Mass where he'd left off.

Leland Edwards, on the other hand, maintains his enthusiasm for teaching all his life. But, having served under the misdirected leadership of the numbskull Dean (and later President) Zastrow for twenty-five years, Leland realizes, upon Zastrow's retirement, that no one is better suited to take over the leadership of Rookery State College than he is, and so, despite his desire to remain a classroom teacher, he reluctantly agrees to finish out his career as president.

I think the same fortitude can be found in Rachel in
The Love Hunter and Peggy Benoit in *Rookery Blues.*
Rachel's vocation, until the end of the story, is being the
faithful caregiver of her husband Larry, who is dying a
slow death from multiple sclerosis. Of the five main characters in *Rookery Blues*—all five are college instructors—
Peggy strikes me as the least flawed, although now that I
look behind the profane bluster of Victor Dash, the
union organizer, I can't find much fault with him either.

Conversely, apart from the many fools who populate
my novels, I believe I have brought at least four downright
bad people to life. Two of them seem to have not a single
redeeming feature. Like Shakespeare's Iago, they appear
to have been born to be self-serving and to confound
everyone they come in contact with. I'm talking about
Judge Bigelow and Tom Pearsall in *North of Hope,* whose
overriding ambition it is to saturate the Indian reservation
with illicit drugs.

Two others, while they commit despicable acts, I find
myself sympathizing with when I try to understand what
motivates them. Wallace Flint in *Grand Opening* is
friendless and trapped by his epilepsy in the village he
longs to leave. Imogene Kite in *Dear James* envies Agatha
McGee's honored place in the town of Staggerford, a
station in life that she will never attain. So it's thwarted
ambition and jealousy that drive these two to the point
of extreme frustration. Perhaps if I had delved into the
backgrounds of Tom and the judge, they might not

have turned out to be so thoroughly bad. But because they come onstage fully formed, with no secrets or hidden motives behind them, I have developed no sympathy for them.

It's easier, of course, to portray bad individuals than good. There are so many ways to be bad, whereas the good seem to be converging on a single path to virtue. That's why I was extremely flattered a few years ago to read, in a review of my work, that my novels are unusual in that they make good people interesting.

10

summing up

Why are some people naturally good, while others have to overcome obstacles to goodness? There seems to be no answer to this question. Twenty-five years ago I used as the epigraph of my first novel this passsage from the fiction of John Cheever: "Oh why is it that life for some is an exquisite privilege, while others must pay for their seats at the play with a ransom of cholers, infections, and nightmares?" Cheever's subject isn't precisely goodness—it's happiness—but his conclusion is the same as mine, namely, that we seem simply born to be the people we are, or our formation takes place so early in life that there's no recalling it.

The goodness of people such as Grandmother Elizabeth, Father Adrian Lawrence, and my dying, twelve-year-old friend Jackie seems to flow effortlessly out of their souls, while in others, such as Father Frank Healy, Simon Shea, and Miles Pruitt, we see a harder-won type of goodness. Even the upright Agatha McGee has to overcome a great deal of resentment in order to forgive Imogene Kite in *Dear James*.

In truly bad people, on the other hand, there seems to be no obstacle to bad behavior, no better nature to overcome. Evil seemed to flow just as effortlessly out of Timmy Musser, the nine-year-old terrorist, as goodness flows from Father Lawrence. Of the three worst characters in my fiction—Wallace Flint in *Grand Opening* and Judge Bigelow and Tom Pearsall in *North of Hope*—none is delayed from carrying out his dastardly deed by even a millisecond of ambiguous thought.

One way to take the measure of goodness is to look at the way various people handle their vocations. I think of the two priests in *North of Hope*. While the elderly Adrian Lawrence leads his life of loving-kindness, impervious to doubts and difficulties, Frank Healy goes about his duties despite suffering through a dark night of the soul. "I've sprung a very big leak and my spirit is draining away." Working under this strain, Frank Healy's service to others strikes me as the more heroic sort of goodness.

In *The Dean's List,* Angelo Corelli seems blessed with an almost superhuman supply of good will. He goes happily and effortlessly about his work, spreading cheer along Administration Row—even in committee meetings, for which he has an unnatural affection. His greatest admirer is Leland Edwards: "If I'm ever to become as lighthearted as I've always secretly wished to be, it will no doubt transpire through my association with Angelo Corelli, a man of irrepressible good humor. Even on occasions such as today when his silliness is inappropriate and irksome, you can't help envying his bubbly chemistry and wishing you'd been born under a star like his."

(I remember the day Angelo Corelli stepped into my imagination. Feeling the need to brighten up *The Dean's List,* I invented his character while listening to a concerto by his namesake, Archangelo Corelli, which, like all of his compositions, is a piece of such clarity and brightness and grace that I was moved to create a human counterpart to the music.)

But one doesn't find these vocational contrasts only in fiction. I recall how easily my father went about his duties in the grocery store, indeed how easily and seemingly unimpeded he slipped through his eighty-seven years on this earth. On the other hand I think of Jim Powers, who made writing seem like an opponent to be defeated.

By contrast, I thank God that my vocations have been such a joy for me. In my forty-two years of teaching, I never grew bored or disappointed in my students. In my thirty years of writing, I haven't had a single day of writer's block, and although my rate of production has diminished in recent years—due primarily, I think, to a Parkinsonian decrease in stamina—I still approach the word processor with a feeling of excitement every morning.

My happy days, in other words, have far outnumbered the unhappy ones. It's a commonly held belief that happiness stems from attitude rather than outward circumstances in the world. If this is true, I believe I can trace my happy attitude back to my earliest years, when, as a little boy, I looked out and saw the world from the security of that all-important cocoon of goodness, my parents' love.